REVISE EDEXCEL FUNCTIONAL SKILLS LEVEL

Information and Communication Technology

REVISION GUIDE

Series Consultant: Harry Smith

Author: Alison Trimble

TASK FILES
Some of the tasks in this book ask you to work with task files. Go to this webpage to download the task files:
www.pearsonschools.co.uk/ICTdownloads

To revise all the topics covered in this book, check out:

Revise Functional Skills Level 2

Information and Communication Technology Workbook   9781292145907

THE REVISE SERIES

For the full range of Pearson revision titles, visit:
www.pearsonschools.co.uk/revise

Contents

A small bit of small print

Edexcel publishes Sample Assessment Material and the Specification on its website. This is the official content and this book should be used in conjunction with it. The questions in Now try this have been written to help you practise every topic in the book. Remember: the real exam questions may not look like this.

Preparing for your test

The Level 2 Functional Skills ICT test will assess your ability to use a computer and software efficiently, safely and securely. Make sure you know what to expect in the test.

The tasks

The test is divided into two sections:

Section A

- **Task 1:** Use the internet to find and select information.

Section B

- **Task 2:** Process numerical data and produce graphs and charts.
- **Task 3:** Use the correct software to produce a document for a specific audience and purpose, using information from the files provided and your own ideas.
- **Task 4:** Compose an email with a message and an attachment.
- **Task 5:** Using ICT - managing your computer.

The files

You'll be given some computer files to work with, including:

- a folder of images
- a text file
- a spreadsheet
- a Microsoft® Word document called **ResponsesL2XXXXX**.

Getting it right

You will only have access to the internet for the first 15 minutes of the test. Make sure you complete Section A in that time and check you have got all the information you need.

Evidence

The test paper will include some boxes with the heading **Evidence**. These boxes tell you how to present your answers. You might need to print out a document or a screen shot, or type something into the **ResponsesL2XXXXX** document. You should label any printouts clearly with your name, candidate number and centre number in the footer.

Screen shots

For some tasks, you'll need to take a **screen shot** (an image of your screen).

1. Press the 'Print Screen' key to save a screen shot to the Clipboard.
2. Open a Microsoft® Word document.
3. Right-click anywhere in the document and select 'Paste'.
4. Save the document with a sensible name.

Questions about using ICT

You will also be asked some general questions about ICT. You need to know about:

- staying safe online
- protecting data
- choosing appropriate software
- health and safety
- using ICT to work with others
- using system settings
- storing and backing up files.

Planning your time

You will have **2 hours** to gain a maximum of **50 marks** in the test. You should spend:

- 15 minutes on **Section A**
- 1 hour and 45 minutes on **Section B.**

Remember to use any time left at the end of the test to carefully check your answers.

Now try this

- Open a blank Microsoft® Word document and save it in a new folder on your desktop.
- Go to uk.pearson.com
- Paste a screen shot of the website into your blank document.

The basics

In the test you will need to demonstrate that you have a basic knowledge of computers.

What you need to know

You need to know how to do the following:

- start up your computer, log in and shut down properly
- use the features of Windows® **Desktop,** including the icons, Recycle bin, taskbar and notifications area
- use Windows® **Search** to find an application, such as Microsoft® Word, open it and close it again
- move and resize windows, including using the 'Minimise', 'Maximise' and 'Restore' options.

Input and output devices

Input devices are items of hardware that **send** information to a computer.

Output devices **receive** data from a computer.

Some devices can be both. An ordinary monitor is an output device, whereas a touch screen, such as an interactive whiteboard, allows you to input instructions as well.

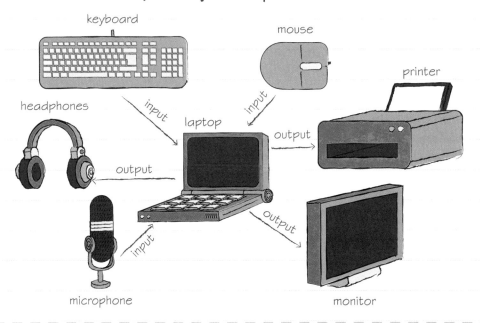

keyboard | mouse | printer | headphones | laptop | microphone | monitor

Hardware and software

Hardware is the word for the physical parts of a computer and other devices connected to it. Examples include: monitor, keyboard, mouse, printer, microphone and tablet.

Software is data or instructions for the computer that are stored electronically. You can't see or touch software, but it makes your computer work. Applications and operating systems are types of software.

Getting it right

In the test, you'll need to choose the right software for the task. This guide uses:

- Microsoft® Word for word processing tasks, such as creating posters and leaflets
- Microsoft® Excel for tasks involving spreadsheets and charts
- Microsoft® PowerPoint for creating presentations.

Now try this

You have a printed photo you want to email to several friends. What input device could you use to put it on to your computer?

Problem solving

From time to time, you may experience problems when using your computer. Here are some potential solutions to help you if this happens.

Solving common problems

If something goes wrong in the test, don't panic! Look at the following common problems and their solutions.

> I accidentally deleted some text.

 Click the undo button to **undo** the last changes you made.

> I was working on a document in Microsoft® Word and my computer shut itself down before I could save it.

 Microsoft® Word regularly **autosaves** and will offer to recover your file when you reopen the application.

> I deleted the wrong file.

 Open the **Recycle Bin**. Right-click on the file and select 'Restore'.

Getting help in the test

In the test, you can only use the internet in **Section A**, and are not allowed to ask for help with the tasks. However, you can use Windows® Search and Microsoft® Office offline Help in Section B. To access this:

 Click the question mark icon at the top right of the window.

 Click the drop-down arrow and choose 'Word help from your computer'.

Getting it right

If something goes wrong with your computer during the test, you won't be expected to fix it. Raise your hand and let the invigilator know.

 Don't spend too much time using help features during the test. Make sure you prepare well, so that you know what you need to do and where everything is.

Now try this

- Use the offline help in Microsoft® Word to find instructions for inserting a text box.
- Paste a screen shot of the 'Help' window in a new Microsoft® Word document.
- Save it on your desktop with a suitable name.

Settings and accessibility

Many of the settings on your computer can be changed to make it easier for you to use. Make sure you know how to use the test computer comfortably and with ease.

The Control Panel

You can change settings in the **Control Panel**.
Type 'control panel' into the Windows® Search bar and select it on the results panel.

- Choose 'Mouse' to swap the buttons over if you are left-handed, or to change how quickly you need to double-click.
- Choose 'Display' to change the size and text of icons.
- Choose 'Speech Recognition' to use your voice to control the computer. This option can help someone who has impaired vision or who finds the keyboard hard to use.

Useful tips

- Use keyboard shortcuts if you struggle to use the mouse.
- Change the colour or size of the text to make it easier to read.
- Use the slider bar in Microsoft® Office applications to zoom in or out.

> — ────|──── + 100%

The Ease of Access Centre

The **Ease of Access Centre** brings together all the settings in the Control Panel that could help make the computer more accessible.

Find it using Windows® Search or through the Control Panel. Make sure you know how to:

✓ use the Magnifier

✓ turn on Narrator, which reads aloud the options in dialogue boxes

✓ change the colour and size of the mouse pointer

✓ choose a High Contrast theme.

There are a wide range of settings that are designed to help people with visual, hearing and motor impairments use technology more easily.

Golden rule

If you're using a shared computer, especially at work, check with the person responsible for IT before changing any settings to be sure that other people won't be affected.

Settings within applications

You can also make individual applications more accessible, too. Search 'accessibility' in the help feature of the individual application. In Microsoft® Office applications, you can adjust the colour and size settings, and add keyboard shortcuts.

Go to page 3 for more on getting help.

Now try this

Simon is visually impaired and struggles to read the options in a window.
Identify **two** features in the Ease of Access Centre could help?

Health and safety

It is important to know how to minimise the risk of health problems associated with using computers. You also need to be aware of safety hazards and how to prevent accidents.

Are you sitting comfortably?

Your posture (the way you sit) is important. Poor posture can strain muscles and joints. Make sure your work station is set up correctly.

Wear glasses if you are supposed to.

Make sure your elbows are at greater than 90° to the desk, and your wrists are supported.

Sit with your back straight, shoulders relaxed and lower back supported.

Keep your feet flat on the floor, or use a foot rest if they don't reach.

Adjust brightness of monitor to avoid eye strain.

Adjust the position of your monitor to avoid glare and reflections.

Make sure your eyes are level with the top of the monitor and about 50–80 cm away. Use a monitor stand if necessary.

Make sure there is no clutter under desk and move all wires safely out of the way.

What else can you do?

- 👍 Tell your optician if you use a computer a lot so they can test your eyes at the correct distance.
- 👍 Take regular breaks to avoid muscle strain and injuries, such as Repetitive Strain Injury (RSI).
- 👍 Look away from the screen frequently to avoid eye strain and headaches.
- 👍 Look out for hazards, such as trailing wires and plugs that could overheat.

What the law says

Under the Health and Safety at Work Act, an employer must provide equipment that is safe and comfortable to use.

Golden rule

Never consume food and drink near the computer. Crumbs in the keyboard may mean a costly repair, and a drink spilled on electrical equipment could put people's lives at risk.

Now try this

Rachel spends a lot of time working on her computer and is worried about how this might affect her health. List **six** pieces of advice you could give to help Rachel stay safe and healthy.

Files and folders

You should already know the basics of working with files and folders. For Level 2, you also need to know about other storage methods, such as removable storage, cloud storage and compressing (or zipping) files.

Backing up

If you have important data on your computer, it is a good idea to store a copy in another place. There are lots of reasons to back up your files.

- Your computer could be lost or stolen.
- A virus might destroy or damage your data.
- Files could be deleted accidentally, or deliberately by hackers or malware.
- The computer could develop a fault or be damaged.

Go to page 7 to revise keeping your computer safe.

Cloud storage

Cloud storage services, such as Microsoft® OneDrive allow you to store files online. There are advantages and disadvantages associated with storing files in 'the cloud'.

- 👍 You can access your files from any device with internet access.
- 👍 It's easy to share files with others.
- 👍 You can easily work on a document with other people.
- 👍 Your files are safe if something goes wrong with your computer or you lose your removable storage.
- 👎 You can't access your files while you're offline unless you've saved them on your computer as well.

Zipping and unzipping

Zipping **compresses** a file or folder so that it takes up less storage space and can be sent and received faster.

You can attach a zipped folder to an email. (You can't attach a folder to an email.)

Zipping files

1. Right-click a closed folder.
2. Choose 'Send to Compressed (zipped) folder'.

You'll see an identical folder with a zipper icon – the original is unaffected. You can zip an individual file, too.

Unzipping files

1. Right-click a zipped file or folder.
2. Choose 'Extract All'.
3. Choose where to save the extracted files.
4. Click 'Extract'.

Removable storage

You can store files on a computer itself or use a range of **removable storage devices**. The main types are:

- external hard drives
- CDs, DVDs and Blu-Ray Discs™
- USB memory sticks.

They can be used to **backup** important files, or **transport** files to another computer. You can move files and folders to and from removable storage devices by using copy and paste or drag and drop.

Getting it right

If you're asked for a screen shot of your files in the test, take a screen shot to show the whole folder.

Now try this

- Move the files **AugustNewsletterPG06L2** and **SeptemberNewsletterPG06L2** into a new folder on your desktop called **Newsletters**
- Zip this folder and rename the zipped folder **ZippedNewsletters**

Keeping your information safe

You need to know how to protect your computer from malware, such as viruses.

Malware

Malware is 'malicious software' designed to change or steal your data or alter the way your applications work. Malware can affect your computer in lots of ways.

- **Viruses** can slow down your computer, stop applications working, or even send emails from your account.
- **Adware** may load pop-up ads on your screen, or even replace your home page with adverts.

If you share files, send emails or are part of a network when you are infected, you could pass the malware on to others too.

Protecting against malware

- Install antivirus software, such as Norton AntiVirus™ or AVG AntiVirus™, and keep it up-to-date.
- Make sure your computer automatically installs Windows® Updates.
- Don't download files from untrustworthy websites.
- Don't open attachments in suspicious emails.

Go to page 26 to revise staying safe online.

Passwords

Passwords are a good way to keep your information safe. You can use passwords to protect your whole computer, your emails and social media, and individual files. Never tell anyone your passwords and avoid writing them down anywhere.

Golden rule

A strong password should:

- ✓ contain a mixture of letters, numbers and symbols
- ✓ contain both upper case (capital) and lower case letters
- ✓ be at least 8 characters in length
- ✓ be memorable to you, but not easily guessed.

Choosing a strong password

You should use strong passwords that are easy for you to remember, but difficult for others to guess. Choose something memorable to you and then change some of the letters to make it harder to guess.

- 👍 If you support Manchester United, you could try adding some capital letters and numbers: M4NUn1t3d
- 👍 If your father's name is Peter, you could add the year of his birth and some capital letters: pETEr62

Stay secure by changing your passwords regularly.

Now try this

1 Name **two** types of malware.
2 Identify **two** ways you can pass malware on to other people.
3 Emily works at Estrick College. Which of these would make the best password for her work email account?

  (a) emily   (b) college
  (c) EsTricK   (d) EsTr1ckC01

Putting it into practice

You will use skills covered in this chapter for every task in the test. The test paper may also include one or two specific questions about using ICT. When you answer this kind of question, make sure you do the following things.

✓ Read the question carefully.

✓ Be specific.

✓ Look at how many marks are available and include the same number of points in your answers.

✓ Check your answer.

 State **one** example of each of the following:

- input device
- output device
- input and output device.

(3 marks)

 You only need to think of one example for each bullet point. Don't waste time thinking of more examples than you need.

 You accidentally delete an image in a file you are working on. What should you do?

(1 mark)

 State **three** ways you can protect your computer from malware.

(3 marks)

 Identify **two** characteristics of a strong password.

(2 marks)

 Be specific! It isn't enough to just answer 'Contain a mix of letters'.

State what the Narrator in the Ease of Access Centre does.

(1 mark)

 In the test, if you couldn't remember what the Narrator does, you could make an educated guess based on what the word means.

State **two** situations in which you might want to compress (zip) a folder.

(2 marks)

 Don't panic if you can't think of two answers — one could still get you a mark.

The internet

In Section A of the test, you will need to find and select information on the internet. You will also need to know the difference between the web, a web browser and a website.

What is the internet?

The **internet** is a network of computers and devices all over the world, connected by cables and wireless technology. A **website** is a set of files, called **web pages**, stored on **web servers** across the world.

You can access the internet through a **broadband** connection or through mobile services, such as **4G**.

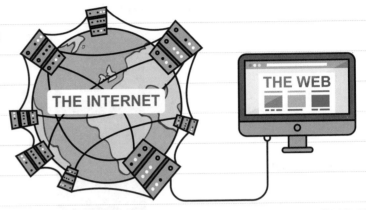

What can you use the internet for?

People use the internet every day at work and at home for many reasons, including:

- searching for information
- communicating via email or video calls
- playing games
- shopping
- listening to music
- watching TV or films.

What is the web?

The **World Wide Web**, or **the web**, is the name for a collection of **websites** that can be accessed via the internet.

Websites are made up of **web pages**.

Each web page has a unique web address. For example, www.pearson.com

Go to page 10 to revise navigating a website.

What is a web browser?

To view web pages and move between them, you use software called a **web browser**. Examples include:

- Microsoft® Edge
- Google Chrome™
- Mozilla Firefox®
- Safari®.

You need to type a website address exactly, or the web browser won't be able to find it.

Now try this

Your friend emails you a link to a web page. You click the link but the web page does not load.
- Give **two** possible causes for this problem.
- For each cause, suggest a possible solution.

Navigating a website

You need to know how to use the features of a website to move around it and find information.

Website navigation features

Your web browser has many useful features to help you move around the internet.

Click this plus sign to open a new **tab**.

Tabs allow you to keep one website open while you visit another in the same window.

Use the **navigation arrows** to move forward and back through web pages.

Type key words in the **search box** to find things quickly.

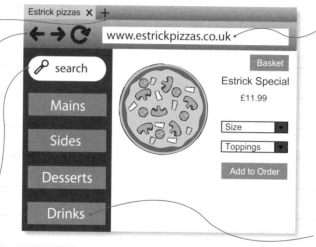

Type a **URL** (website address) in the address bar. Website addresses begin **http://** or **https://** (secure sites). This is often (but not always) followed by **www**.

Click a **hyperlink** to go to another page. Text hyperlinks are often a different colour or underlined. Pictures can be hyperlinks too.

Finding information

To search for a word or phrase on a web page, hold Ctrl and F on your keyboard to open the **Find** box. You can copy text from a web page just as you would in Microsoft® Word.

Saving files

Some websites may have files for you to download, such as a restaurant menu, a form or a bus timetable.

To save a file from a web page, right-click the file then select 'Save Link As', 'Save Target As' or something similar, depending on your browser and what it is you're downloading. Make sure you save the file where you will be able to find it.

If you can't find a file that you have downloaded from the internet, go to the browser menu and click 'Downloads'.

Hyperlinks

You can right-click or left-click hyperlinks:

- left-clicking takes you to a new page
- right-clicking gives you two choices: open the new page in a new tab, or open the page in a new window.

Favourites and bookmarks

Use **Favourites** (in Microsoft® Edge) or **Bookmarks** (in Google Chrome™) to store links to pages you want to go back to later. In both browsers, click the star to add a favourite or bookmark.

Go to page 13 to revise evaluating information on the internet.

Now try this

You want to compare the price of the book 'The Great Gatsby' on two different websites.
- Search for a website that sells books.
- Find the price of 'The Great Gatsby'.
- Open a new tab and search for a different website so that you can compare the price of the book.

Searching for information

Task 1 in the test requires you to do an internet search. You will have 15 minutes for this task. You will be asked to save some information to use later in the test.

What is a search engine?

Search engines search the web for information. The search results consist of links to different web pages that include the **search terms** you have typed in. Some examples of search engines are Google® Web Search, Microsoft® Bing and Yahoo® Search.

Efficient searches

Choose efficient search terms to get the best results for your search. Follow these tips to improve the efficiency of your internet search.

* Use a few important words only.
* Don't worry about the order of your search terms.
* Don't worry about capital letters and punctuation.

Advanced searches

* Use "−" to filter out unwanted results. For example, to find a recipe for an omelette without mushrooms, you could search: 'recipe omelette −mushrooms'.
* Use quotation marks before the first word and after the last word to find an exact phrase. For example, "Petra's Pet Palace" shop.
* Use **OR** to search for similar words at once. For example, 'hamsters OR gerbils'.

Providing evidence

If you're asked to paste a screen shot of your search and the results into the 'Responses' document, the screen shot should show:

✓ the search engine you used
✓ the words you searched for
✓ the top of the list of results.

Make sure you give the address of the web page and not the address of the search engine results.

1 Click the hyperlink in the search results to go to the website.
2 Copy the address from your browser bar.

Now try this

* Use an internet search engine to find the name of the castle in the Ribble Valley in Lancashire and the postcode of its museum.
* Take a screen shot showing the name of the search engine and the search criteria you used.
* Paste the screen shot into **ResponsesPG11L2** and complete the table with the required information.

Searching for images

In Task 1 of the test, you could be asked to find an image and save it to use later.

Searching for images

To search for images, click the 'Images' link at the top of your search engine page. The rules for efficient searches apply to images as well as information.

Using images

Even if you have permission to use an image, it's important to provide **acknowledgement**. You should always credit the owner.

Getting it right

In the test you don't need to worry about finding copyright-free images. You are acknowledging the source by pasting the web address into the 'Responses' document.

Providing evidence

In the test you will need to show evidence of your image search. You could be asked to:

- copy and paste the image into your 'Responses' document: Right-click the image and select 'Copy image', then paste it into your document

- save the image file: Right-click the image and select 'Save image as'. Type a suitable file name and save the image to the Desktop

- give the web address of the image. Click the image to go through to its web page, then copy the address from your browser and paste it into your 'Responses' document.

You should only insert a single image and not an image gallery into the 'Responses' document.

Finding images you can legally use

Images are usually protected by copyright. You can use filters to find images that you can use without breaching copyright. You should still always check for any terms of use and acknowledge the owner of the image.

In Google Images™:
1. search for an image
2. click 'Search tools'
3. click 'Usage rights'
4. select 'Labelled for reuse'.

In Microsoft® Bing:
1. choose 'Images'
2. search for an image
3. click 'License'
4. choose 'Free share and use'.

Go to page 11 to revise using efficient search criteria.

Now try this

1 What do you need to include if you use images you find yourself in the test?
2 List the **three** steps you would follow to copy an image into your 'Responses' document.

Evaluating information

Information found on the internet can come from any source and may not always be reliable, unbiased, up-to-date or relevant. In your test, you will need to evaluate all of these things to decide whether information is fit for purpose.

Is the source reliable?

Anyone can create websites and publish information on the internet. In your test, you need to distinguish between reliable and unreliable sources.

Who is the author?

- Is he/she an expert in the subject?
- Is he/she associated with a reputable, official organisation?
- Is there any contact information so you can ask about the sources used?
- What is his/her purpose?

The most reliable websites are usually set up by official organisations and companies. These websites can be identified by their web address.

Web addresses

You can often identify reliable webpages from their web address.

Web address ending	Source
.com	commercial organisations
.org	not-for-profit organisations
.co.uk	UK company's website
.gov	government organisation
.ac.uk or .sch.uk	universities, schools and colleges

Is the information up-to-date?

Information may have been reliable and accurate when written, but if it is not updated regularly, it may become out of date.

- Look for a **last updated** date.

  Last updated: *25th August 2012*

- Check whether the content refers to past dates as though they are in the future, e.g. "We are planning a great event for August 2013."

- Look for copyright information at the bottom of the page. There should be a year mentioned.

  ©2016. All rights reserved.

Is the source objective?

If the writer is giving you **facts**, or presenting both sides of a debate fairly, they are **unbiased**. If they are trying to persuade you to do something or are just sharing their opinion, they may be **biased**.

Is the information relevant?

Make sure the source you choose has relevant information for the question you are asked. Underline key words in the question to help you focus your search. For example, if you are asked to find a contact number, you shouldn't give an email address instead.

Now try this

Rafiq works at a hotel in Manchester. A guest at the hotel would like to buy tickets for a circus that's coming to town. Evaluate these search results and decide which one Rafiq should choose.

(a) Circuses in Manchester Throughout History
(b) Save our City Blog: Stop the Circus
(c) Foxtail Circus: 2013 show a sell-out!
(d) The Manchester Visitor Information Centre

Staying legal

Many of the articles, images, and audio and video files you can find on the internet are protected by copyright law. You don't need to be a legal expert but you do need to be aware of **copyright law** and **The Data Protection Act**.

Protecting information

1 **Copyright law** protects producers of written work, music, video, software and images. It is illegal to use copyrighted material without permission.

2 **The Data Protection Act** is a law which affects organisations that store personal information on a computer or in paper files. It states that personal data stored by organisations must be:

- necessary
- accurate and up-to-date
- stored safely, e.g. in locked filing cabinets or protected by a strong password
- available to the person on request.

What is protected by copyright?

© If you can't see a copyright symbol on something, it doesn't mean you are free to use it in your own publication. Always assume something is protected by copyright unless you can find evidence that it isn't. Copyright-free material includes material that is:

- in the **public domain**, which means you can use it freely. This is usually because the copyright has expired.
- made available for reuse by the copyright owner, for example, using a Creative Commons (CC) license. There are often restrictions on how the material can be used.

Plagiarism

Plagiarism is the act of taking someone else's work and pretending it is your own. Doing this is a breach of copyright law. Examples of plagiarism include:

- copying part of an article you find on the web and including it in a report you are writing
- including a photo on your blog from another website and labelling it: 'Here's a photo I took yesterday.'

What can't you do with copyrighted material?

Copyright law prohibits you from doing the following with someone else's work:

- copying it
- distributing it
- displaying it
- modifying or adapting it.

Golden rule

If you are in any doubt about whether something is protected by copyright, you should contact the owner or seek further advice.

Getting it right

In the test, you won't have time to check whether an image or other file is copyright-free. You are acknowledging the source by providing the web address of where you found it.

Now try this

Tasha is setting up a customer database and must comply with the Data Protection Act. Give **three** pieces of advice to help her to stay legal.

Putting it into practice

In the test, you'll need to find and select accurate, relevant, unbiased information on the internet and provide evidence of your search. You could also be asked about how to reuse information legally, following copyright law and The Data Protection Act. Look at the following tasks to see what kind of things you could be asked in the test.

 You may use the internet for this section only.

Open **ResponsesPG15L2**

(a) Use an internet search engine to find an image of Picasso.

Take a screen shot of the search engine showing the criteria and the search results you used.

> Underline the key words in the task so you know exactly what you're searching for.

Paste the screen shot into **ResponsesPG15L2**

Complete the table in **ResponsesPG15L2** with a copy of the image and the website address.

(b) Use the internet to find:

- the name of the city where Picasso was born

- the year that Picasso completed the painting *Guernica*.

> The web address you give as evidence mustn't be the search engine page. Go right through to the actual website to find the full address.

Complete the table in **ResponsesPG15L2** with your answers.

Resave **ResponsesPG15L2**

Evidence

A completed copy of **ResponsesPG15L2**

(6 marks)

> Go to page 1 to revise how to produce screen shots.

- -

 State **three** things you need to consider when evaluating information you have found on the internet.

(3 marks)

What is email?

You may already be familiar with sending and receiving emails, attaching documents and saving the files you receive. At Level 2, you need to be aware of the two different types of email. You should also be able to consider the advantages and disadvantages of email compared to other ways of communicating.

Types of email

There are **two** main types of email. Both types of email give you your own email address, and a mailbox where you can store messages you receive and compose messages to send.

 An **email client** is an application that you install on your computer. One example is Microsoft® Outlook, which comes as part of the Microsoft® Office package. You can use it offline to compose messages, and then send them later when you have an internet connection.

 Web-based email services use the web, so they can only be accessed from computers with an internet connection, such as Gmail™, Microsoft® Outlook.com and email accounts provided by internet service providers. There's no software to install as you send messages from a website using your web browser.

Both types give you your own email address and a mailbox where you can store messages you receive and compose messages to send. Sometimes, in a business, more than one person may share an email address, such as customerservice@example.com.

Advantages of email

- 👍 You can access a web-based account anywhere and on any device when you have access to the internet.
- 👍 Emails usually arrive in a few seconds and can be sent any time of day or night.
- 👍 You can keep a permanent record of what has been said, unlike a phone call.
- 👍 You can send an email to lots of people at the same time.
- 👍 You can attach documents to share with other people.

Disadvantages of email

- 👎 The recipient of an email needs access to the internet to receive it.
- 👎 An email sent to one person can be easily forwarded to many others, including people you wouldn't want to see it.
- 👎 Malware is easily transmitted via email.
- 👎 People can be deceived by phishing emails.
- 👎 You don't always know whether your email was received and read, unlike an answered phone call.

Go to page 26 for more about how to stay safe online.

Now try this

Mitsuko needs to contact all the plumbers who work for her company to ask them to come into the office for an urgent meeting at 4.30 p.m. today. List **three** advantages and **three** disadvantages of using email instead of phone calls to let them know.

Sending and receiving emails

In the test, you'll be asked to prepare an email with an attachment that you've already edited or created. Even if you're confident sending and receiving emails, here are some points to revise.

Creating an email

If you are using Microsoft® Outlook:

1 Click 'New Email' to start a new message.

2 In the test, you'll be given an email address to send your email to. This must be copied exactly into the 'To:' box.

3 You must add a relevant subject in the 'Subject:' box, stating what the email message is about.

4 Attach the correct document.

5 Include a relevant message.

Replying and forwarding

When you receive an email, you can respond in several ways.

- You can reply to the person who sent the email by clicking 'Reply'.
- You can reply to everyone the email was addressed to by clicking 'Reply All'.
- You can send the email to a person who didn't receive the original email, by clicking 'Forward'.

Golden rule

In your test, you're only allowed to use the internet for the first 15 minutes, while you complete **Section A**. So, for the email task, you will need to use an email client - usually Microsoft® Outlook—as it can be used offline. Make sure you know how to use Microsoft® Outlook.

Getting it right

In the test, you won't actually send the email, but you will be asked to take a screen shot of it. Make sure everything listed on the left is visible.

Now try this

- Prepare an email to your manager, sven_goerdensson@example.com, asking for his feedback on a business letter you have drafted.
- Attach the file **LetterPG17L2**
- Paste a screen shot into a new document.
- Give the document a suitable file name.

Email contacts

A contacts list is your email address book – a directory of the people you send emails to and receive emails from. You could be asked to use it in the test.

Saving a contact

You can add people to your **contacts list** so you don't have to type out their address every time you email them.

1 Right-click their email address in an email you've received from them. Choose 'Add to Outlook Contacts'.

2 Add a name in the form that opens. You can include other details, such as a phone number, company name and an address.

3 Click 'Save & Close'.

Adding a new contact

You could be asked to store an email address you've been given in the test.

1 Click the 'Contacts' icon (at the bottom left of the screen) and choose 'New Contact'.

2 Add the relevant details to the form.

3 Click 'Save and Close'.

 Many services will automatically remember contacts you email regularly, and complete the address for you when you begin to type it.

What is Cc?

Cc is short for 'carbon copy', an old method for making more than one copy of a paper letter. Use Cc if you want someone to receive the message, but not necessarily do anything about it.

Go to page 14 to revise the Data Protection Act.

What is Bcc?

Bcc means 'blind carbon copy'. If you put an email address in this field, the person will receive the email but the other recipients won't know. You can use Bcc to protect people's privacy and avoid breaching the Data Protection Act. For example, if you wanted to send the same email to multiple customers efficiently and legally.

Now try this

For each of the following scenarios, identify which address field you should use (To, Cc or Bcc).

- You are sending an email to a customer and you want your boss to see the message.
- You are sending an email to your boss.
- You are sending the monthly newsletter to all the customers.

Searching and sorting

You need to know how to search and sort an email inbox in Microsoft® Outlook (or other email clients) and how to sort emails in different ways.

Searching emails for a keyword

If you have hundreds of emails, scrolling down to find a particular one could be very time consuming. Use the **Search box** instead.

Make sure you use **efficient search criteria**, as you would when you are using an internet search engine.

Search criteria terms

- 'Monday' would find all the messages with the word Monday in them.
- 'Monday OR Tuesday' would find all the messages with **either** of those words in.
- 'Monday AND Tuesday' would find only the messages with **both** of those words in.
- "Monday morning" (using speech marks) would find only the messages containing that **exact phrase**.

Other searches

When you click in the Microsoft® Outlook Search box, a Search Tools ribbon will appear. You can use the buttons on this ribbon to search in more advanced ways.

- You can click the paperclip symbol to display only emails with attachments.
- You can choose which folders you want to search in.
- You can search by sender, subject, date received, recipient and more.

Go to page 11 for more on efficient searches.

Sorting your inbox

Microsoft® Outlook normally displays emails in date order, with the most recent at the top, but you can sort them in other ways. For example, you could reverse the order to show oldest emails first, or you could sort by sender or size.

To change the way your emails are sorted:

1. left-click on 'Arrange By:' at the top of the Email viewing pane

2. choose what you want to sort your emails by.

You can arrange dates by 'Newest on top' or 'Oldest on top', and names by 'A on top' or 'Z on top'.

Arrange By: Date

✓	Date
	From
	To
	Categories
	Flag: Start Date
	Flag: Due Date
	Size
	Subject
	Type
	Attachments
	Account
	Importance
	Show as Conversations
✓	Show in Groups
⚙	View Settings...

Now try this

You have 1,200 emails in your inbox. You need to find the first email you had from one of your customers, Joanna. How could you use email search features to find it?

Organising emails

If you receive a lot of emails every day you need to know how to keep your inbox organised.

Using folders

Instead of having all your emails together in your inbox, you can create separate folders. For example, you might keep all emails about a certain project or from a particular client in one folder.

Creating a new folder

1 Right-click the folders area and select 'New Folder' from the drop-down menu.

2 Give your new folder a suitable name.

3 Drag-and-drop the emails you want into the new folder.

You can also move emails between folders using the 'Move' icon.

Sorting them by subject or sender might help you find the emails you want.

Using rules

Once you have created folders, you can create **Rules** so that Microsoft® Outlook automatically puts new emails in the correct folder for you.

1 On the 'Home' tab, click 'Rules', then select the 'Always Move Messages...' option.

2 Choose which folder you'd like those emails to go to, and click 'OK'.

3 Repeat for each subject or sender you want to keep separate.

Go to page 19 to revise searching your emails.

Junk email

Often called **spam**, this is all the email you probably don't want to see, such as advertisements and scams.

Email applications recognise a lot of emails as spam and divert them into the 'Junk email' folder of your mailbox. You can change the way the filter behaves by using the 'Junk email' options.

Golden rule

You should check your Junk email folder regularly in case the filter has caught any emails you want to see.

Deleted emails

You can delete one or more selected emails using the 'Delete' icon. This doesn't free up storage space – the emails simply move to the 'Deleted Items' folder. To empty this folder, right-click it and choose 'Empty Folder'.

Don't worry if you accidentally delete an email.
1. Open the 'Deleted Items' folder.
2. Right-click the email and select 'Move'.
3. Choose 'Inbox'.

Now try this

1 You missed an important email from your Managing Director because you received multiple emails all at once. How could you set up Microsoft® Outlook to prevent this from happening again?

2 Your junk email is automatically deleted after one week. Why might this be a problem?

Getting emails right

It is important to write a suitable message containing relevant information with a formal tone in emails. You will need to use correct spelling, grammar and punctuation in your email in the test.

Using the correct language

When you are sending an email to someone you don't know, you should:

- write clearly and in full sentences
- punctuate properly, with full stops and capital letters
- avoid using text message language
- avoid using emoticons.

Your spelling is not being tested, but what you've written must make sense. You are allowed to bring a dictionary into the test, but try not to use it too much because it will take up valuable time.

Getting it right

If you are asked to attach a file to your email in the test, make sure you mention it in the email message. For example, 'I've attached my draft poster. Please let me have your comments.'

Golden rule

After you have written an email, you should read it carefully to check for mistakes or typos. Don't rely on the spelling & grammar check because it may not pick up grammar and punctuation errors.

Greetings and sign-offs

Use a greeting beginning with 'Dear.' followed by either a first name, or a title and surname.

✓ Dear Varinder

✓ Dear Mr Singh

✗ Dear Mr Varinder Singh.

If you don't know the person's name, use 'Dear Sir or Madam'.

It isn't appropriate to start a business email with 'Hi' or similar.

It is important to end your email with a sign-off. You can finish an email with 'Regards' followed by your name. If you have asked someone to do something in the message, you can sign off the email with 'Thanks'.

If you send a lot of formal emails, you can save time by setting up an automatic email signature.

Choosing a subject

The subject is the first thing a receiver sees, so it is important to make it effective and professional. Make sure it is:

- relevant to the email
- brief, so it is quick and easy to read
- free from language and punctuation that might look like spam.

Here are some good and bad examples:

✓ Tomorrow's meeting

✓ Monthly targets for September

✗ Hello!

✗ Sale! Save £££££!

Now try this

You have created a new logo for your company.

- Compose an email to send to the company's Print Manager, Max Green, asking whether it is suitable for printing on company stationery. His email address is max@example.com.
- Attach the image file **NewLogoPG21L2**
- Paste a screen shot of your email into a new document, and save it with a suitable file name.

21

Email risks

Email has advantages over letters and phone calls, but there are also risks you need to be aware of and you need to know how to avoid them.

Phishing

Phishing emails pretend to be from your bank or other commercial sites that hold your bank or credit card details. If you click on the link in the email, you'll be asked to enter your login details, which someone can then use.

What if I think it might be genuine?

 Go directly to the relevant website by typing its address and check your account. If in doubt contact your bank's fraud helpline.

Malware

Emails containing **malware** may look as though they have come from a friend or a trusted business. However, clicking the link in the email or opening an attachment may download malware to your computer.

What if I think it might be genuine?

 Contact the sender by phone or using an email address you know is genuine.

Scams

Some junk emails are **scams** asking you to pay money into an account. For example, the email may appear to be from a friend who has a problem abroad and needs money, or from a company saying that you have inherited a large sum and need to pay a fee to receive it.

> Go to page 7 to revise keeping your information safe.

Other risks

 You could breach the Data Protection Act by sending personal information to an incorrect or shared email address.

✓ Check email addresses carefully. You could also password-protect attached files and give the intended recipient the password by phone or text.

 It's easy to send, reply to or forward an email too hastily. There is an option to recall a message, but the recipient may already have read it.

✓ If in doubt, save it to review later.

Now try this

Describe **three** email risks you need to be aware of, and how you can protect yourself against them.

Email troubleshooting

At Level 2, you need to know how to fix some common problems with emails.

Stuck in the Outbox

If you're online when you click 'Send', your email normally goes straight away and a copy appears in your 'Sent items' folder. Sometimes you may notice that an item is stuck in your 'Outbox'. If this happens, check that you are online.

You could also try clicking 'Send and Receive'.

Sending large files

You can only send files up to a certain size by email. If your attachment is too large, it won't send. Your email service will usually warn you if this happens.

To avoid problems with sending large attachments, you can:

- zip the files to compress them
- use a cloud storage service to share the files instead of sending them by email.

Go to page 6 to revise cloud storage and zipping files.

Bouncing back

If an email can't get through to its recipient, it will **bounce back** and you will receive a message saying it couldn't be delivered. This could be for several reasons.

- **The recipient's mailbox is full**. If so, you should contact them another way to let them know.
- **The email address doesn't exist.** This could be because the recipient has changed jobs, or may just be a spelling mistake! Check you have typed the address accurately, then contact the company if necessary.
- **The recipient has set up an out-of-office response.** Don't worry – your email will be waiting for them when they return.

Problems with attachments

If the recipient has an older version of software than the one you're using, they might not be able to open the files you have sent them. A potential solution is to re-save the file in a different format.

 In Microsoft® Office applications, click 'File', then 'Save As'.

 Choose a suitable format. For example, in Microsoft® Word **.doc** files are designed to work with older versions of the application.

Now try this

You want a colleague to add information to some draft documents you've created, but your email account won't send them because the files are too large. What could you do instead? Suggest **two** possible solutions.

Had a go ☐　Nearly there ☐　Nailed it! ☐

Putting it into practice

For **Section B: Task 4**, you will be asked to prepare an email. After creating your email, always make sure that you check the following.

✓ The email address is spelled correctly.

✓ The subject is appropriate.

✓ The attachment is the correct document.

✓ The message makes sense and includes all the required information.

✓ The language is appropriate, and spelling and grammar are correct.

Alana, the regional manager of your hairdressing salon, has asked you to send her a fact sheet on split ends for customers of the Queen o'Cuts hair salon chain.

You will need to use Microsoft® Outlook in offline mode for this task, not a webmail service such as Gmail™.

In Microsoft® Outlook, on the 'Send/Receive' tab click 'Work Offline'.

- Prepare an email to the sender, attaching a copy of the file named **FactsheetPG24L2**

- Include a message telling Alana you have attached the file and ask her for feedback.

Alana's email address is:

alana_queenocuts@example.com

Proofread your work carefully, especially the email address and subject line. The spell check will not check these for you.

- Produce a screen shot showing the email you have prepared, and paste it into a document.

- Save the document with an appropriate file name on the Desktop.

Evidence

- A screen shot of the email that you have prepared.

- Make sure it clearly shows the email address, the subject, the message and the attachment.

- Make sure the screen shot is clear and large enough to be read.

(4 marks)

Online tools

You need to know a little about online tools: apps and services that enable people to communicate, collaborate and share information, such as sound, images, video, messages and documents.

Communication tools

Effective communication is essential in any business or organisation. Social media websites, instant messaging services and video conferencing software, such as Skype®, allow people around the world to communicate in real-time.

Businesses use these online tools for external communication with a variety of different purposes, such as:

- advertising goods and services
- communicating with staff and customers
- providing customer support
- finding new clients and customers.

These online tools can also be used for internal communication within businesses to facilitate teamwork and encourage team bonding.

Go to page 6 for more about cloud storage.

Collaborative tools

File storage services, such as Dropbox™ and WeTransfer™, allow people to store and share files.

Cloud-based file storage services, such as Google Drive™, allow people scattered across the country or across the world to work together on stored files: music, documents, spreadsheets – anything.

Cloud-based file storage services enable users to set permissions that determine whether people can edit documents, or just view or download them.

These tools mean that there is no need for documents to be emailed back and forth. Users can also be confident that they have access to the latest version of the document at all times.

Advantages of online tools

- 👍 You can easily share resources with other people.
- 👍 Businesses can improve internal and external communication.
- 👍 Cloud-based file storage services enable you to save space on your computer.
- 👍 You can be sure you are working on the latest version of a document.
- 👍 You can access your documents anywhere.
- 👍 Your documents will automatically be backed up.

Disadvantages of online tools

- 👎 You need to be connected to the internet.
- 👎 Syncing and downloading files can take a long time.
- 👎 You can't guarantee the security and privacy of files and information you store online.
- 👎 Web-based office suites tend to have less advanced formatting options.

Now try this

You've produced a draft human resources policy, which you need to share with the company's regional HR managers, who are based all over the UK. The HR managers need to be able to check and edit the draft at the same time to finalise it. How could you use online tools to solve the problem?

Safe and savvy online

The internet is an incredibly useful resource that keeps us all connected, but it is important to know how to keep yourself and others safe online.

Staying safe online

Follow these tips to stay safe online.

- ✓ Have **strong passwords** on social media accounts, and keep them secret.
- ✓ Make sure your **online friends** are people you know in real life. Remember that photos on social media may not be genuine.
- ✓ Don't put **personal details** on your public profile. This information could be used for identity theft.
- ✓ Report any online **bullying, threats** and **harassment**.
- ✓ Use the **privacy settings** on social media accounts to make sure only your friends can see your posts and profile.
- ✓ Set up **parental controls** to protect young people from seeing unsuitable websites.
- ✓ Use your email account's **junk filter** to avoid receiving emails you don't want to see.

Go to page 7 for more on passwords and viruses.

Netiquette

When we're online, it can be easy to type something that we wouldn't say to someone's face.

You should follow these rules of behaviour.

- Treat others with respect, even if you don't like their views.
- Do not post angry messages. This is known as trolling.
- Avoid typing in all capital letters – it's considered to be shouting.
- Keep posts brief and check they make sense.
- Think twice before posting something on the internet. Remember, once something is on the internet it can be around the world in seconds, copied via email and posted on social media sites.

Suspicious emails

Never reply to emails that ask for personal details, such as your login to a website or your bank details.

If you receive an email with an unexpected link, don't click it. If you know the person who sent it, ask them what it is first. If you don't know the person who sent it, it's best to delete the email.

Now try this

A new employee has started working at your firm. He isn't your friend on social media but you can see his profile, including photos and a post where he has given a friend his mobile number. Suggest **two** pieces of advice you could give him.

Putting it into practice

Your test may include one or two general questions about using ICT. At Level 2, you'll be expected to write a few short sentences rather than one-word answers.

✓ Read the question carefully.

✓ Look at how many marks are available and include the same number of points in your answer.

✓ Use specific terminology and descriptions.

✓ Check your answer.

 1 You need your manager to approve a training video you've made for apprentice plumbers, but the video is too large to send by email.

Name **one** online tool you could use.

Give **one** advantage of using this tool.

(2 marks)

> Always pay attention to the command word in the question. It will give you a clue about how to answer.
>
> If you are asked to **name** something, you can give a short, one-word answer.

 2 Name **one** online tool you could use to hold a meeting with managers in different parts of the world.

State **one** advantage of using this tool.

(2 marks)

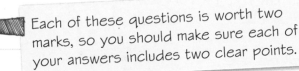

> Each of these questions is worth two marks, so you should make sure each of your answers includes two clear points.

 3 Your friend is worried about keeping his information safe and private on the internet.

Identify **two** pieces of advice that you could give him about using the internet safely.

(2 marks)

> Often there will be many possible answers to a question. Don't try to list them all. Give as many as the question asks for.

Entering text

Microsoft® Word is a **word processing** application. It is used for documents that mostly involve text, such as posters, flyers, reports, essays, letters, memos and forms.

Opening Microsoft® Word

To open **Microsoft® Word**, type 'word' into the search box, and click on the app.

Double-click the **Blank** template option to start a new document.

Getting it right

If you're familiar with Microsoft® Publisher (desktop publishing software), you can use it in your test to create a poster or flyer.

Your keyboard

Make sure that you know where these keys are on your keyboard.

Press the Caps Lock key, to type all things as uppercase.

Use the tab key to move the cursor forward.

Press the Delete key to erase text to the right of the cursor.

Press the backspace key to erase text to the left of the cursor.

Hold down either Shift key to type a capital letter.

The Control key (Ctrl) is used with the Alt and Delete keys to open the Task Manager.

Press the Space bar to move the cursor one space forward.

Press the Enter key to start a new paragraph.

To use the symbols above the numbers, hold down the Shift key at the same time.

Adding and deleting text

To add text, click anywhere on the document to make the cursor (|) appear and start typing.

To delete text, one character at a time, use the Delete or Backspace key. To delete entire words, sentences or paragraphs, click and drag to highlight the text you want to delete and press the Delete key.

Using Microsoft® Notepad

In your test, you might have to copy and paste text from a Microsoft® Notepad file. Microsoft® Notepad is a simple text editing application. It doesn't allow you to apply formatting, so you will need to copy the text into Microsoft® Word and produce your document there. Maximise the Microsoft® Notepad window to ensure sure you select and copy all of the text.

Now try this

- Open the file **NewsletterPG28L2**
- Select and copy all the text into a new Microsoft® Word document.
- Correct the spelling errors and delete any text that shouldn't be there.

Formatting text

Formatting means changing the way text looks – its size, style and colour. It is used to emphasise important information or to make your page more attractive and interesting.

You need to know how to:

- change font style and size, such as from Times New Roman size 14 to Comic Sans size 8
- use **bold**, underline, *italics* and highlighting
- change font colour
- change the case to CAPITAL LETTERS.

Golden rule

Avoid using WordArt: you need to demonstrate that you can use a range of text formatting techniques.

Selecting text

Remember to select text before you try to change its format.

- To select a word, double-click it.
- To select a paragraph, double-click in the left margin next to it.
- To select all the text in your document, triple-click in the left margin.
- To select part of a sentence or paragraph, click and drag the cursor across the text, or click at the beginning then hold down the Shift key and click at the end of the selection.

Choosing a font

You should use the same font for all of the main text in your document.

✓ Choose an easy-to-read **sans serif** font, such as Arial or Calibri. Avoid serif fonts, such as Times New Roman.

✓ You can choose a different font for the title and subheadings but make sure it is appropriate and don't use more than one.

Serifs are the decorative tips on the ends of letters in some fonts.
Times New Roman is a serif font.
Arial is a sans serif font.

Top tips for formatting

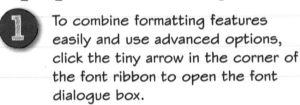

1 To combine formatting features easily and use advanced options, click the tiny arrow in the corner of the font ribbon to open the font dialogue box.

2 To quickly copy formatting from one selection of text to another, use the Format Painter.

Getting it right

In the test, you need to make sure any formatting is suitable for the audience and purpose. Revise the formatting that suits different types of document so you don't spend too much time on this in the test.

Now try this

Open the file **NewsletterPG29L2** and make the following changes.

- Format all of the text in a **sans serif** font.
- Apply suitable font sizes to the title, subtitle and subheadings.

Your work must fit on one A4 sheet.

Page layout

You need to know how to use layout features to improve the appearance of documents.

Layout basics

Templates

When you open Microsoft® Word, you'll see a selection of templates to choose from. For the test, use the 'Blank' template.

Page borders

To add a page border, choose the 'Design' tab and click 'Page Borders'. Select an 'Art' border from the drop-down menu and click OK. There are also 'Box' borders, which are useful for business documents.

Margins

To change the size of the margins, choose 'Margins' on the 'Page Layout' tab. You can select one of the predefined options, or you can set 'Custom Margins'.

Orientation

To switch the layout of your paper from portrait to landscape, choose the 'Page Layout' tab at the top of the window and click 'Orientation'.

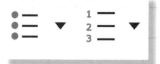

Lists

If you have a list of short, linked points, you can format them as bullet points. If your list items are in a particular order, for example a set of instructions, you can format it as a numbered list.

To create a new set of bullets, click the 'Bullets' icon and type the first line. Press the Enter key for each new bullet.

1 Highlight the lines you want to add bullet points to and click the 'Bullets' icon.

2 To add a new bullet point on the next line, press the Enter key.

3 To end the list, click the icon again.

You can make a numbered list in the same way using the 'Numbering' icon, which is next to the 'Bullets' icon.

Headers and footers

In the test, you'll be asked to put your name, centre number and candidate number in the footer on all of your files.

1 Choose 'Footer' on the 'Insert' tab.

2 Select the three column layout and type in your details.

3 When you have finished typing, click 'Close Header and Footer'.

Alignment

You can use the alignment buttons to position text to the left, in the centre or to the right of the page.

Now try this

- Open the file **LayoutPG30L2**
- Change the orientation to landscape.
- Split the **Audit** paragraph into four bullet points.
- If necessary, adjust the document to fit onto one A4 sheet.

 To fit the document onto one A4 sheet, you could either delete blank lines or resize the text.

Using tables

You can use tables to present numbers, facts and figures in an organised way that makes them easy to read. Tables are often used in informative documents, such as fact sheets, reports and leaflets.

Using tables to present information

✓ Use tables to make facts and numbers stand out.

✗ Avoid putting long chunks of text in a table.

✓ Your table should help make your document clear and easy to read.

Make sure your table is easy to understand by including the following things:
- a suitable title
- column headings and row labels
- formatting that makes important cells stand out.

Rows and columns

To **change** the width of a column or the height of a row:

1. move your pointer over the boundary between two columns or rows until it becomes a resizing symbol
2. click and drag to change the column width or row height.

To **insert** a row or column:

1. right-click a cell in the row or column next to where you would like to insert a new one
2. from the drop-down menu, choose 'Insert' and then select the relevant option.

To **delete** a row or column:

1. select all the cells in the row or column you want to delete
2. right-click and select 'Delete Columns' or 'Delete rows'.

There are other ways to do this – use the method you're comfortable with.

Formatting and layout

You can change the font and alignment in your tables as you can with ordinary text. You can also add a background colour to rows, columns and individual cells.

To make formatting changes, use your mouse to highlight the contents of the cell, row, or column you want to change. A toolbar will appear.

To change the background colour, click the paint tin icon. Your table might be easier to read if you make alternate rows a different colour.

Moving tables

You can move a table around the page by dragging it, using the crossed arrows in the top left corner.

Customer ID	Name
0001	Dave Arnold
0002	Jordanna Rothman
0003	Harold McGee
0004	James Beattie

Now try this

- Open the file **TablePG31L2**
- Format the table so it is clear and easy to read.
- Save the document with a new file name.

Using images

In the test, you could be asked to place an image in a document. Read the question carefully to work out where you can find the image. You'll be given a folder containing some images, but you could be asked to use an image you found on the internet in Task 1.

Inserting an image

There are two ways to **insert** an image into a Microsoft® Word file.

- If the image is saved on your computer, go to the 'Insert' tab and select 'Pictures'.

- If the image is from the internet or another file, copy and paste it directly into your document.

Make sure your images don't hide or overlap with any text.

Resizing and rotating

To **resize** or **rotate** an image, first click on the image to show its handles.

Use the circular handle above the image to rotate.

Use the corner handles to resize.

Golden rule

Always use the corner handles to resize an image. Otherwise, you might distort it.

Cropping an image

You might want to **crop** an image to remove unnecessary parts or blank space.

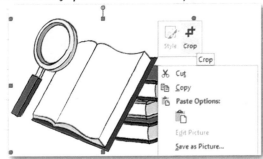

1 Right-click the image to bring up the formatting tool bar.

2 Click the 'Crop' icon.

3 Move the cursor over a cropping handle. The cursor will become T-shaped. Click, hold and push inwards to crop the image.

Using the Layout Options

You can use Layout Options to position and arrange images in your document. The default setting is **In Line with Text**. To change the position of your image, select it, click the Layout Options icon and choose:

- **Square** to wrap text around your image
- **Tight** to wrap text closely around an image
- **In Front of Text** lays the image on top of the text or in a blank space.

Go to page 30 to revise page layout.

Now try this

- Open the file **ImagesPG32L2**
- Insert the image file **LogoPG32L2** in the top right of the page.
- Copy and paste the image **AlarmClockPG32L2** under the heading **Audit**

 You will need to crop both images.

Using text boxes and shapes

You can improve the appearance of a document by using text boxes and shapes.

Text boxes

If you want to position some text in a particular bit of space in your document, or label a diagram, one useful option is to use a text box.

Built-in

Simple Text Box

 Click roughly where you want the text box to be, go to the 'Insert' tab and choose 'Text Box'.

 Click the 'Simple Text Box' to add it to your page.

 Replace the sample text with your own.

 Remember to drag the text box to where you want it to be.

Resizing and rotating text boxes

Resizing and rotating text boxes is just like working with images, except that you don't need to worry about distorting the dimensions.

- Use the corner handles or the side handles to resize.
- Use the circular handle above the image to rotate.
- Click the 'Layout Options' icon to change how the text box fits with the other text on the page.

Go to page 32 to revise Layout Options.

Shapes

Shapes can make your document look more attractive. They are especially good for flyers and posters.

 Select 'Shapes' on the 'Insert' tab

 Click the shape you want to use

 Click on the page then drag the cursor to draw the shape

 Right-click and choose 'Add Text'.

Changing the appearance of text boxes and shapes

Select the 'Format' tab to display formatting options for textboxes and shapes.
For example, you can change the fill colour and the border. You can use 'Layout Options' to change the way textboxes and shapes behave in the document, just as with images.

Don't use too many colours in your design. Stick to dark text on a light background so that the document is easy to read.

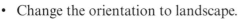
Now try this

- Open the file **ShapesPG33L2**
- Change the orientation to landscape.
- Move the last line, which begins 'Finally…', into a suitably formatted text box.
- Add a shape with the words 'Summer Edition' in the top left-hand corner.

Audience and purpose

When you create a document, make sure you consider the **audience** and **purpose**. You should choose formatting and layout features that are appropriate for the type of document and the audience it is aimed at.

Types of document

Here are some examples of documents you could be asked to create in the test:

- newsletter
- fact sheet
- poster
- advert
- leaflet
- invitation
- flyer
- letter
- report
- meeting minutes.

Formal or informal?

Always consider the **audience** (who the document is for). Does the document need to be formal or informal? As well as using appropriate language, you should use appropriate formatting.

In a formal document:

- choose plain sans serif fonts
- use mainly black and white, with a few colours if appropriate
- use tables to display information clearly.

In an informal document:

- use colours (but not too many) to make the document more appealing
- choose more interesting fonts (but make sure they are still easy-to-read).

Designing for a purpose

Always think about the **purpose** of the document.

If a document is intended to provide information, such as a report or a letter:

- focus on presenting the information in a simple, professional way
- make sure all the information the reader needs is included.

If a document is intended to attract attention, such as a poster or a flyer:

- use a range of font sizes – larger for posters as they have to be read from a distance
- use colour and images to make it eye-catching
- keep the text short and simple.

Getting it right

Make sure that any formatting features that you use are there for a reason and enhance the document. Think about how your document would look printed out.

- Have you used dark text on a light background?
- Does the design fill the page?
- Is the font easy to read?
- Is the title a sensible size?

Go to pages 35-37 to revise different types of documents.

Now try this

A colleague has typed up the minutes from a staff meeting. Review the file **MinutesPG34L2** and list **six** changes that would make the document more suitable for the audience and purpose.

Posters and adverts

You could be asked to create a poster or an advert. The main purpose of these documents is to attract attention and provide key information.

Features of a poster or advert

headings larger than body text

formatting techniques, such as colour and shapes attract attention (not WordArt)

large font sizes to allow text to be read from a distance

★ **Dinglewood Canoe Club** ★

Do you want to try something new?

Canoeing is a fun way to keep fit and make new friends. Come along to our friendly club and give it a try. Your first session is <u>free</u>!

All ages and abilities are welcome. Canoes and lifejackets provided.

Meetings: every Saturday at 11.30 am At Dinglewood Water Centre

For more information email: Ravi@Dinglewoodcanoe.co.uk

suitable image, sensibly positioned and sized

text enhancements, such as underline and bold, are used to highlight key information

no large areas of empty space

Document size

You may be asked to produce a document at a particular size, for example A4, or A5. To change the page size, use the 'Size' button on the 'Page layout' tab.

If the option you need isn't listed, choose 'More Paper Sizes...' then select 'Custom Size' and input the page dimensions you need.

You can also create non-standard sizes by adjusting margins or splitting the page into two columns.

Getting it right

Read the question carefully and follow all of the instructions. If the question gives you a layout plan to follow, make sure you use it!

Go to page 34 to revise audience and purpose.

Now try this

Create a poster for the window of your hairdressing salon to attract models.
The poster should include:
- text from the file **CompetitionPG35L2**
- the image file **FlowersPG35L2**

Create a poster that is clear, easy to read and suitable for its audience and purpose.
Add your own text to encourage people to apply.

Remember to check for spelling errors and remove any text that isn't needed.

Newsletters, leaflets and flyers

You could be asked to create a newsletter, factsheet, flyer or leaflet. The main purpose of these documents is to provide information in an attractive way.

Features of a newsletter, leaflet or flyer

text formatting, such as bold and colour, used to add visual appeal

headings larger than body text

no large areas of empty white space

more information than a poster

images positioned neatly next to relevant text

Trip to Rome

Culture Club trip
Every year the Beecham College Culture Club organises a trip to Europe, and this time we're going to Rome in Italy!

Why Rome?
Rome is packed full of amazing history and culture. We'll visit famous sights like Roman Coliseum, the beautiful Sistine Chapel, and the Vatican.

Key information
- Monday 2nd – Saturday 7th March (Easter Holidays)
- £150 per person
- Price includes flights from Beecham Airport and accommodation
- Pay in three instalments

How to sign up
Come to our meeting:

Sports Hall
Wednesday 23rd January
4.30 pm

Or for more information email:
Katie@cultureclub.ac.uk

There is also lots of delicious food to try! Pizza, pasta and ice cream are just some of the traditional Italian foods available.

formatting techniques, such as bulleted lists and columns, used to present information clearly

headings and subheadings used to break text into sections

Using columns

You can use columns to make large sections of text easier to read. Columns are most appropriate for newsletters and leaflets.

 Select the text you want to format in columns.

 On the 'Page Layout' tab, click 'Columns'.

 Choose the number of columns you'd like.

To undo column formatting, select the text, then set the number of columns to one.

Leaflet layouts

You might need to think about how a leaflet would be folded. For example, to create inside pages of a leaflet made from a folded side of A4, you could create a landscape A4 document and format the text into two or four columns.

Now try this

Make sure the images are positioned in appropriate places and don't overlap the text.

- Open the file **LeafletPG36L2**
- Change the layout to landscape.
- Format the text into three columns.
- Insert the images **HairBrushPG36L2** and **HairStylesPG36L2**
- Format the leaflet so it is clear and easy to read, and suitable for purpose and audience.

Letters and business documents

You could be asked to create a letter or other business document. The main purpose of a letter or business document is to communicate information in a simple and professional way.

Features of a letter or business document

Letters need to be formatted in a specific way. When you create a letter, make sure you include all of these features.

recipient's address on the left

a formal greeting, starting with 'Dear' and one of:
- recipient's first name
- recipient's title and surname
- Sir/Madam.

text organised into paragraphs and left-aligned

Caleb's Cake Creations

23 High Street
Beecham
Northshire
NR2 0QA

The Big Cake Fair
30 Taylor Street
Estrick
ES3 9ZP   19/07/2016

Subject: Stall at The Big Cake Fair

Dear Sir/Madam,

I'm writing to apply for a stall at the upcoming Big Cake Fair in Estrick. I set up Caleb's Cake Creations three years ago, and since then we have gone from strength to strength. At first I made all the cakes myself, but thanks to high demand I now have a team of three bakers and an apprentice working with me.

We specialise in making children's birthday cakes. Last year, we won the gold medal in the children's celebration cake category at the Northshire Baking Championships, as well as Best Creative Design at the UK Bakers' Society Competition. Please find enclosed some photographs of our work.

Caleb Cake Creations would be a colourful and exciting addition to the Big Cake Fair, and the stall would help us make valuable contacts in the industry.

Yours faithfully,

Caleb Wilkinson
Director, Caleb's Cake Creations

---

sender's address in the top right corner

today's date

a subject line to say what the letter is about

- 'Yours sincerely' if you've used the recipient's name,
- 'Yours faithfully' if you have not
- space for a signature
- name and job title of the sender

Meeting minutes and reports

Follow the same principles for other business documents, such as **meeting minutes** or **reports**. For these document types, make sure you format headings to stand out.

Golden rule

Keep formatting simple! You could add a plain border or use a bulleted list, but stick to plain fonts and avoid fancy borders, shapes and unnecessary colour. Leave the text black so that it is easy to read.

Now try this

- Open the file **MinutesPG37L2**
- Copy and paste the text into a new Microsoft® Word document.
- Format the minutes appropriately, including the image file **NewLogoPG37L2** as the logo.

Checking your work

You should always check any work you produce on the computer to make sure it is accurate and suitable for the audience and purpose. In the test, it is also important to check that you've done what is asked.

Key things to check

Here are some key points to look for when checking your work.

 Have you considered your audience and purpose?

 Are the page borders and font style appropriate?

 Is your work all on one page (if it should be)?

 Is the orientation (portrait or landscape) what was asked for?

 Have you added a header or footer if one was asked for?

 Is the layout balanced, or is there too much empty white space?

 Have you included the right images, in the right places?

Spelling and grammar

This isn't an English test, but your work must make sense. Let Microsoft® Word check the spelling and grammar, but make sure you also read any text carefully yourself, too.

 You may need to make something smaller or delete additional space if necessary.

Go to page 29 to revise formatting text.

 You may need to enlarge images or increase the size of headings and body text to fill empty space.

Appropriate formatting

In the test you may be asked to make sure your document is **clear**, **easy to read**, and **informative**. Check that:

- text is a sensible size and in an easy-to-read font
- headings and subheadings are bigger than the body text
- key information is formatted to stand out
- text is not hidden by images or narrow table columns.

Copying text accurately

If you are copying text from a Microsoft® Notebook file, make sure you delete any notes that are there for your benefit, such as a label to show which bit is the title. For example:

✗ This event is held every August [insert the month name you found in Section A Task 1] in Bristol.

✗ This event is held every [August] in Bristol

✓ This event is held every August in Bristol.

Now try this

- Open the file **KitchensPG38L2**
- Use your formatting skills to make sure it is clear, easy to read and fit for purpose and audience.
- Run the spelling & grammar check, then carefully read over your document.

Putting it into practice

For Task 3, you will be asked to produce a document based on text provided in a Microsoft® Notepad file and including information you found in **Section A**, and one or more images. Make sure you:

✓ read the question carefully

✓ follow all the instructions

✓ save files where you can find them, and give them sensible names

✓ check your answers.

You work for a travel agency, called Just Cities. Your manager has given you some text about Barcelona and asked you to make a fact sheet for customers.

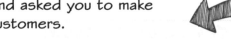

The purpose of a fact sheet is to provide information in an attractive way. Make sure that you use appropriate formatting.

Produce a fact sheet on Barcelona. It must be:

• one A4 page

• clear and easy to read

• suitable for customers seeking holiday information.

It must include:

• the text from **BarcelonaPG39L2**

• the correct logo from the folder **ImagesPG39L2**

The audience for a fact sheet want to gain lots of information quickly and easily.

• three other appropriate images selected from **ImagesPG39L2**

• the information you found in **Section A, Task 1**.

As Task 1 is not part of this practice exercise, the information you need is: 'Las Ramblas'.

Add a short piece of text of your own to encourage people to book early.

Enter your name, candidate number and centre number in the footer.

Save the fact sheet with a relevant file name.

There may be mistakes in the text you have been given. Read the document carefully and check for any spelling errors.

Evidence

A copy of your fact sheet saved on your desktop.

(18 marks)

Understanding spreadsheets

As you may already know, spreadsheet applications allow you to organise, sort and present data, and perform calculations quickly and accurately. This guide uses Microsoft® Excel 2013.

What does a spreadsheet look like?

This is the sort of **spreadsheet** you could be working with in your test. It shows a shop's weekly takings for the different categories of goods it sells.

Each box in the grid is called a 'cell'. Every cell has a 'reference', which is made up of the letter of its column and its row number, e.g. D5. If you click on a cell, the reference appears in the 'name' box.

Tables should always have a suitable heading.

The row labels (in Column A) are usually formatted differently to the column headings.

Column headings are formatted to make them stand out.

You can add a worksheet to your workbook by clicking the + icon. You won't be expected to use this feature in the test.

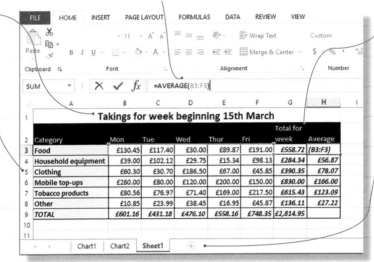

Workbooks and worksheets

Files that you create in spreadsheet applications are called 'workbooks'. Workbooks contain worksheets, which you can see in the bottom left corner of the screen. You can move to a different worksheet by clicking on the tab.

Go to pages 58–61 to revise producing graph and charts.

What can you use spreadsheets for?

Spreadsheets are useful for many different purposes. They are useful for managing a lot of numbers, for example:

- keeping track of your personal budget
- creating an invoice
- tracking scores at a sports event
- storing the results of a survey.

Now try this

- Open the file **ClothingPG40L2**
- Change the name of the worksheet **Monday** to **Sales**
- Add two more blank worksheets to the workbook, named **Budget** and **Profits**
- Rearrange the three worksheets in the order **Budget, Profits, Sales**
- Save the workbook with a new name.

Entering and changing data

You need to be able to enter data into a spreadsheet and change data that's already there.

Entering data

You can **enter** data by clicking on a cell to select it and typing. To move to a different cell, you can use the mouse to click on a new cell, or use the arrow keys on your keyboard to move there.

Changing data

If you need to change the data in a cell, you can:

- click on the cell to select it and start typing to replace all the contents of the cell

- double-click the cell to get a flashing cursor and edit the numbers or letters

- click in the formula bar, which shows the contents of the active cell, and type to change the contents.

| B3 | ▾ | : | ✕ ✓ fx | Thursday |

	A	B	C	D	E
1	Daily Report				
2					
3	Monday	Thursday	Wednesday	Thursday	Friday
4					
5					

Copying and pasting cells

To copy a cell, select the cell and do one of the following:

- hold Ctrl and C on the keyboard
- click the 'Copy' icon on the ribbon
- right-click then select 'Copy' from the menu.

The cell will be surrounded by a moving border. You can press Esc to cancel.

To paste the contents in another cell, select that cell and do one of the following:

- Hold Ctrl and V on the keyboard.
- Click the 'Paste' icon on the ribbon.
- Right-click then select 'Paste' from the drop-down menu.

Cutting and pasting cells

You can cut and paste a cell instead of copying it. This moves the contents of the cell, leaving the original cell empty. To cut a cell, select the cell then either:

- hold Ctrl and X on the keyboard
- click the 'Cut' icon on the ribbon
- right-click on the cell then select 'Cut' from the menu.

If you just want to paste the data and not the cell formatting, select 'Values'.

- Open the file **ClothingPG41L2**
- The figures in the **Men** and **Ladies** columns of the **Liverpool** row have been incorrectly entered. Swap them around using copy and paste.

You will need to copy and paste one of the figures somewhere else first.

Rows and columns

For the spreadsheet task, you could to be asked to add and/or delete rows and columns. You may also need to resize rows and columns to make sure that none of the text or data is truncated.

Adding columns and rows

1. Select the column or row immediately after where you want to add a new column or row.

2. Right-click on the grey bar and choose 'Insert'.

Deleting columns and rows

1. Select the column or row.

2. Right-click on the grey bar and choose 'Delete'.

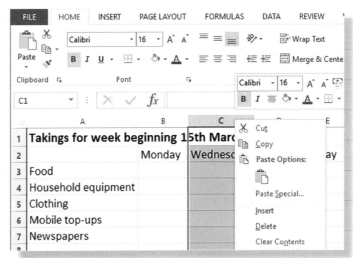

Adjusting height and width

You should always adjust the size of your rows and columns to fit your data.

1. Select the column or row.

2. Drag the border to increase or decrease the height of width.

3. All rows except the heading row should be the same depth.

Another way to make all the text visible is to change the formatting. Select the cell, row or column and click 'Wrap Text' on the ribbon.

Multiple columns

Columns with the same type of data should be the same width. To change the width of multiple columns, select all of the columns and either:

- drag the border between any two columns
- right-click and choose 'Column Width' to select an exact width.

Getting it right

Spreadsheets need to be clear and easy to read. Make sure that none of the text or data is cut off.

Now try this

- Open the file **StaffPG42L2**
- Adjust the column widths so that all column headings and row labels are visible and columns B to G are the same width.
- Adjust column H to a suitable width.

Formatting data

You need to be able to format data in a spreadsheet so that it is clear and easy to read.

Formatting key information

You should use formatting to make key information stand out.

- Increase the size of the title, e.g. 14 pt.
- Make column headings and row labels bold.
- Make averages and totals bold and italic.
- Change the fill and font colour of headings, labels, totals and averages.
- Add a border around key data or all the data.

Formatting cells, rows and columns

1 To apply formatting to a cell, select the cell and use the formatting options on the 'Home' tab.

2 To apply formatting to more than one cell, click and drag to highlight the cells and select the formatting option.

3 To apply formatting to an entire row or column, click the grey bar and select the formatting option.

Formatting numbers

You can display numbers as percentages, dates and currency by applying number formats in Microsoft® Excel.

If there are dates in spreadsheet, you can present them as a short date (15/01/2016) or long date (15 January 2016).

1 Select the cells you want to format.

2 Click the arrow next to 'General' on the 'Home' tab.

3 Select the format you want to use, for example currency.

You can also change the number of decimal places showing, and separate thousands with a comma by selecting 'More Number Formats'.

If you see ##### in a cell after you apply formatting to it, the cell isn't wide enough. Widen the column to see the data.

Getting it right

In the test, you should format the data after you've completed the other steps. Check that formatting is consistent. Avoid unnecessary formatting, such as using too much colour.

Now try this

- Open the spreadsheet **CottagesPG43L2**
- Use text and number formatting to make the data clear and easy to read.

Numbers are normally right-aligned, but you could choose to centre-align a column of single digits instead.

Using simple formulas

You may already know how to use simple formulas to perform calculations such as adding, subtracting, multiplying and dividing. At Level 2, you should also know how to use brackets.

Using simple formulas

1 To start any formula, type an equals sign (=) in the cell you want the answer to appear in.

2 Type the reference of the cell where the first number is, or just click on the cell to put its reference in the formula.

3 Type the maths operator (+, -, *, /).

4 Type the address of the cell where the second number is, or click on its cell.

5 Press Enter to display the answer.

Choosing the correct symbol

Choose the symbols for multiplying and dividing carefully:

/ ✓　　　　÷ ✗

* ✓　　　　× ✗

If you change the number in any of the cells used in the formula, the answer will change, too.

Using brackets

Microsoft® Excel will do multiplication and division before addition and subtraction, unless you use brackets to tell it otherwise. Brackets tell Microsoft® Excel to do the calculation inside the brackets first.

- =A5*B5+2 calculates A5 multiplied by B5, then adds 2
- =A5*(B5+2) calculates B5 plus 2, then multiplies that number by A5

Getting it right

In the test, you may need to include more than one type of calculation within your formula. Think carefully about the order that you write the calculations in as it could affect the answer.

Replicating a formula

Rather than writing out the same formula over and over again, you can **replicate** it. Microsoft® Excel will work out what the cell references in each answer cell should be (although you should check them yourself).

To replicate a formula:

- Click the cell that contains the formula you want to copy.
- Click and hold the black square in the bottom right corner of the cell.
- Drag the cursor to copy the formula into other cells.

Check you only have one cell selected before you replicate!

Now try this

Four friends are planning to hire a car. They will share the cost between them.
- Open the spreadsheet **HirePG44L2**
- Use formulas to calculate how much each friend would have to pay for each vehicle, based on the price plus extras.

Remember to use brackets if you need them.

SUM, MIN and MAX

You can perform calculations in spreadsheet application quickly, easily and accurately using functions such as SUM, MIN and MAX. Functions are ready-made formulas designed to save you time.

Ranges

You need to know how to do a calculation that involves lots of cells, for example finding the total of the cell contents in a column. You can use a **range** instead of typing the cell reference of every cell. For example, B3:B7 includes all of the cells from B3 to B7. You can select a range by clicking and dragging the cursor.

Finding the total

To find the total efficiently, you can use the =SUM function.

 Click in the cell where you want the answer to appear and type =SUM

 Type an opening bracket.

 Select the range of cells you want it to add. Hold down the Control key to select cells that aren't next to each other, to include them in the range.

 Type a closing bracket.

 Press Enter to display the answer.

When to use the =SUM function

Use the =SUM function:

✓ to add a range of cells.

Don't use the SUM function:

✗ to add two numbers together

✗ to subtract two numbers

✗ to multiply two numbers

✗ to divide two numbers.

> ### Golden rule
> Remember, there are no spaces in functions and formulas.

Finding the highest and lowest values

To find the highest or lowest (maximum or minimum) in a set of numbers (a row, column, or any range), Microsoft® Excel has the functions =MAX and =MIN. They are used in exactly the same way as =SUM.

If you are calculating the MAX and MIN values, take care not to include the total!

Shortcuts

Microsoft® Excel has some useful shortcuts to help speed things up.

• Select the cell where you want the answer.

• Click the Autosum button on the 'Home' tab to automatically perform the SUM function. Alternatively, choose one of the other options from the drop-down menu, including MIN, MAX and AVERAGE.

 **Now try this**

• Open the file **TakingsPG45L2**
• Use spreadsheet functions to complete the total for each day.

Averages

Just as Microsoft® Excel has a function to calculate totals, it also has a function to calculate the average, =AVERAGE. However, if a question uses the word average, it doesn't always mean you should use =AVERAGE function.

What's an average?

You may remember from maths lessons that you can find out the **average** of a set of numbers (the mean) by adding them together and dividing by how many numbers there are.

Finding the average

To find the average of a set of numbers:

 click in the cell where you want the average to be calculated

 type =AVERAGE

 type an opening bracket

 select the cells you want to find the average of

 type a closing bracket

 press Enter to display the average.

DATE		× ✓ fx	= AVERAGE (B3:F3)		
	A	B	C	D	E	F
1	Weekend Takings					
2	Category	Friday	Saturday	Sunday	Average	
3	Household equipment	£ 130.45	£ 191.99	£ 89.97	= AVERAGE (B3:F3)	
4	Food	£ 102.12	£ 290.75	£ 97.89		
5	Clothing	£ 117.40	£ 211.59	£ 108.45		
6						

Here, you want to know the average weekly takings for food.

You could replicate the calculation for Food and Clothing by clicking the bottom right corner of the cell and dragging down to highlight E4 and E5.

When not to use =AVERAGE

One of the most common mistakes is using the =AVERAGE function when you have already calculated, or been given, the total for the range of cells. In these circumstances, part of the calculation of the average has already been done. All that's left for you to do is to divide the total by the number of values in the range. Look at the spreadsheet on the right to see an example.

The total weight of the bags has already been found. You just need to divide that by the number of bags to find the average weight.

DATE		× ✓ fx	=C2/B2	
	A	B	C	D
1	Supplier	Number of bags	Total Weight (kg)	Average Weight (kg)
2	Smiths	15	390.69	=C2/B2
3	AJT	40	999.99	
4	GRDS Ltd	60	1450.64	
5	Lots of sand	30	889.75	

Using =AVERAGE wouldn't give you the correct answer.

Now try this

The spreadsheet **DailySalesPG46L2** shows the sales each member of staff in a phone shop made last week.

- Use spreadsheet functions to work out the average daily sales for each member of staff.
- Work out the average daily sales for the staff as a whole.

Finding percentages

In the Level 2 test, you could be asked to work with percentages in spreadsheets.

Percentages

Per cent means out of 100. For example, 10% means '10 out of 100' and is equivalent to the fraction 10/100.

To find a **percentage** of a value in Microsoft® Excel, multiply the value by the percentage. Make sure you include the % symbol.

Percentage cell format

Using percentage format on a decimal will convert it to a percentage and add a % sign. So, 0.2 becomes 20%. It does this by multiplying your number by 100. Don't add a % sign to numbers that are already percentages.

65 formatted as a percentage would give you 6500!

There is a way around this but, if you have a column of percentages in the test, it is enough to simply include the % symbol in the column heading, like this: **Bonus (%)** or you can add the % signs to each one by hand.

Percentage increases

You can **increase** a value by a particular percentage in Microsoft® Excel.

1. Add 100% to the percentage you want to increase the value by.

2. Multiply the value by the total percentage from Step 1. Make sure you use the % sign in your formula.

For example, to add 10% tax to the price of £20 vase:

100% + 10% = 110%.

You would type this in cell C2:

=B2*100%

Percentage decreases

You can **decrease** a value by a particular percentage in Microsoft® Excel.

1. Subtract the percentage you want to decrease the value by from 100%.

2. Multiply the value by that percentage, making sure you use the % sign in your formula.

For example, to work out 30% discount on a dress that costs £60:

100% − 30% = 70%.

You would type this in cell C2:

=B2*70%

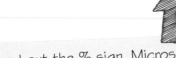

If you missed out the % sign, Microsoft® Excel would multiply £20 by 110, so your answer would be **far** too big!

Getting it right

Always check that your answers make sense:
- Percentages less than 100% are always smaller than the original number.
- Percentages more than 100% are always greater than the original number.

Now try this

- Open the spreadsheet **PricesPG47L2**
- Complete the **Price including VAT** column by adding 20% to the base price.
- Complete the **Price after discount** column to show the price after deducting 5% from the **Price including VAT**

Remember to replicate formulas instead of writing them out multiple times.

Relative and absolute cell references

For Level 2, you need to be able to use relative and absolute cell references when writing and replicating formulas.

What's a relative cell reference?

The address of a cell in a formula is called a **cell reference**. The default type of cell reference is **relative**. For example, B2 in the formula =B2*10% is a relative cell reference.

When you replicate a formula in Microsoft® Excel, it automatically changes the column letter or row number of the cell address in the formula.

- -

What's an absolute cell reference?

In an **absolute** cell reference, the address of that cell will stay the same no matter where you copy the formula.

To write an absolute cell reference, use dollar signs ($) before the letter and the number to 'anchor' the cell address. For example, $F$1 in the formula =B2*$F$1 is absolute, but B2 is relative.

You can use an absolute cell reference if you want one of your values to stay the same each time you do a calculation.

It's important to get the dollar signs in the right place, to the left of the letter and to the left of the number.

To find Wei's commission we need to multiply his sales in B2 by the commission rate in cell F1. The formula in cell C2 is =B2*$F$1

	F1	▾	⋮	✕ ✓ ƒx	10%		
	A	B	C	D	E	F
1	**Salesperson**	**Sales**	**Commission**		**Commission rate**	10%
2	Wei	3112	=B2*$F$1			
3	Sanjit	3850	=B3*$F$1			
4	Dave	2313	=B4*$F$1			
5	Askil	1565	=B5*$F$1			
6						

To find Dave's commission, the address of the sales cell changes to B3, but the commission rate F1 stays the same. The formula in cell C4 is =B4*$F$1

In this spreadsheet, the commission rate is shown in cell F1. It is the same for every salesperson, so you can use an absolute cell reference in the formula.

- -

Now try this

A car salesroom has regular special discounts.
- Open the spreadsheet **CarsPG48L2**
- Use Microsoft® Excel formulas to complete the 'Special offer price' column, including a discount off the prices in column D.

The special offer discount for this week is in cell F2.

Tracking balances

You need to know about spreadsheets that track amounts in different ways, such as running totals and balance remaining.

Running totals

A **running total** tracks the total of a list of numbers and is updated each time another number is added. For example, the amount that has been paid in instalments on an invoice.

The first cell of a running total is the first amount to add. In this example, you would start by typing =B6 in cell C6, to display £30.

	A	B	C
1	R. Stevenson	Invoiceref.	5643RS
	Invoice amount		
2	£235.00		
3			
4			
5		Payment received	Running Total
6	01-May	£30.00	£30.00
7	15-May	£15.00	=C6+B7
8	01-Jun	£15.00	
9	16-Jun	£10.00	
10	25-Jun	£20.00	

For all the other running total cells, add the cell above and the cell to the left. You should type =C6+B7 into cell C7 then replicate the formula in the other cells.

Balance remaining

The **balance remaining** is how much there is left to pay for something.

To calculate this in a spreadsheet, you could use an absolute reference to the invoice amount, with a relative reference to the running total paid.

The formula in cell D6 of this spreadsheet is =$A$2-C6

	A	B	C	D
1	R. Stevenson	Invoiceref.	5643RS	
	Invoice amount			
2	£235.00			
3				
4				
5		Payment received	Running Total	Remaining balance
6	01-May	£30.00	£30.00	£205.00
7	15-May	£15.00	£45.00	£190.00
8	01-Jun	£15.00	£60.00	£175.00
9	16-Jun	£10.00	£70.00	£165.00
10	25-Jun	£20.00	£90.00	£145.00

The formula in cell D9 is =$A$2-C9

Now try this

Your Regional Manager says that your shop sales must be at least £450,000 in the 6 months from March.

- Open the spreadsheet **SalesPG49L2**
- Use formulas to display a running total in the **Cumulative total** column.
- The **Balance outstanding** column must show how much of the target remains to be achieved after each month.
- In B10, display the amount you'll need to achieve in September in order to hit the target.

The September target will be the same as the Balance Outstanding at the end of August.

Conditional formatting

Microsoft® Excel features conditional formatting rules which automatically format certain cells in a particular way.

Conditional formatting

Conditional formatting allows you to make rules that instruct Microsoft® Excel how to format cells in certain situations.
For example, a craftsman wants to highlight all the sales he has made in Manchester in his market stall sales spreadsheet. He does the following:

 Select the names in the Location column.

 Click Conditional Formatting on the Home tab. He then chooses 'Highlight Cells Rules', followed by 'Text That Contains...'

 He types the name (or part of it) in the box, chooses a format from the drop-down menu and clicks OK.

Adding rules

In the 'Home' tab, open the 'Conditional Formatting' menu and select 'Highlight Cell Rules'.

- To apply formatting to values larger than a particular number, select 'Greater than'. On the 'New Formatting Rule' panel, enter the number you want to use and choose how you want the cells to be formatted.
- To apply formatting to dates earlier than a particular year, select 'Less than'. Enter the date of the first day in the year, for example 01/01/1990.
- To apply formatting to cells that contain particular text, select 'Text that contains'.

Editing and deleting rules

Editing a rule

 On the 'Home' tab, click 'Conditional Formatting'.

 Select 'Manage rules...'.

③ Select the rule you want to edit and click 'Edit rule...'.

Deleting a rule

① On the 'Home' tab, click 'Conditional Formatting'.

② Select 'Clear Rules'.

③ Choose an option depending on whether you want to clear all of your rules or just the ones affecting the cell(s) you have selected.

Golden rule

After you apply a rule, always check that it is working as you wanted it to by looking at a couple of cells.

Now try this

- Open the spreadsheet **GymPG50L2**
- Use conditional formatting to highlight all category A members.
- Use different conditional formatting to highlight all dates of birth after 1980.

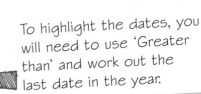

To highlight the dates, you will need to use 'Greater than' and work out the last date in the year.

Using IF

The IF function asks Microsoft® Excel to 'test' some data then do something, depending on what it finds.

What is an IF function?

IF is called a **conditional function** because what Microsoft® Excel does is conditional on (depends on) what it finds. It has three parts:

- What are you testing? (logical test)
- What if it's TRUE? (value if TRUE)
- What if it is FALSE? (value if FALSE)

In a formula you organise it like this:

=IF(logical test, value if TRUE, value if FALSE)

A logical test is a set of instructions that Microsoft® Excel can use to decide what to do in certain situations. It is written using **logical operators**.

Logical operators

Use these logical operators to write your logical test.

Operator	Meaning	Example
=	is equal to	A5="yes"
<>	Is not equal to	A5<>"no"
>	is greater than	A5>100
<	is less than	A5<B5
>=	is greater than or equal to	A5>=B5
<=	is less than or equal to	A5<=B5

Golden rule

To include text in your formula, you need to write it in double speech marks.

How to write an IF function

1 Click in the cell where you want the answer to be and type =IF

2 Type an open bracket symbol.

3 Type your logical test, for example D2>7, followed by a comma.

4 Type what you want the cell to contain if the logical test is true, followed by a comma.

5 Type what you want the cell to contain if the logical test is false.

6 Type a close bracket symbol and press Enter.

Example

This IF formula works out whether the total cost for a booking is more than £200.
If it is, the discount is 20%. If it isn't, the discount is 10%.

| SUM | ▾ | : | ✕ ✓ *fx* | =IF(B3*C3>200, 20, 10) |

▲	A	B	C	D	E	F	G
1	**Fruit Farm bookings**						
2	**Cottage**	**Cost per night**	**Number of nights**	**Discount**			
3	Apple	£35.00		=IF(B3*C3>200, 20, 10)			
4	Damson	£42.00	4	IF(logical_test, [value_if_true], [value_if_false])			
5	Blueberry	£55.00	5				
6	Orange	£75.00	7				
7	Kiwi	£18.00	8				
8							

Now try this

You'll need to include the cost of an item in the charge column if it is required that day.

A bathroom company is holding its annual conference in a hotel. The spreadsheet **CostsPG51L2** shows how much the hotel charges for refreshments, and which days the company requires them.

Use a spreadsheet function to complete the 'Charge' column for each day, based on whether each item is required.

Using VLOOKUP

VLOOKUP helps you look for specific information in your spreadsheet, for example the price of an extra-large T-shirt.

VLOOKUP

The VLOOKUP function searches for values in a spreadsheet list or table.

A VLOOKUP formula has four parts:

- **lookup_value**: what you want Microsoft® Excel to look up
- **table_array**: the table where you want it to search
- **col_index_no**: the column in that table where it should search
- **range_lookup**: enter O

You need to write the formula in this order:

=VLOOKUP(lookup_value, table_array, col_index_no, range_lookup)

If you are going to replicate a VLOOKUP formula, make sure you put dollar signs around the table array cell references to make them absolute references.

Sometimes the table for a VLOOKUP will be on a separate sheet in the workbook. When you need to select the table array, click the tab for the other worksheet, select the table (not any column headings), and complete the last 2 parts of the function. Close the brackets and press Enter to return to the main worksheet.

Example

This spreadsheet shows the membership categories for members of a gym. The fees for each category are stored in a table in cells G5:H7.

You want Microsoft® Excel to look at the membership category, find the associated fee in the table, and place the fee into column E. This is the formula you'd type in E2:=VLOOKUP(C2,$G$5:$H$7,2,0)

	A	B	C	D	E	F	G	H	I	J
1	First name	Last name	Membership category	Age	Fee					
2	Joe	Bibby	A	23	=VLOOKUP(C2,$G5$5:$H$7,2.0)					
3	Charllote	Crichton	A	61	VLOOKUP(lookup_value, table_array, col_index_num, [range_lookup])					
4	Sanjit	Patel	B	29			Category	Fee		
5	Zinnia	Flores	C	45			A	£52		
6	Nevill	Parr	B	36			B	£38		
7							C	£25		
8										

Go to page 48 to revise absolute and relative cell references.

Now try this

A receptionist at a gym has a spreadsheet with member details. She wants an easy way to find a member's date of birth from their membership number.

- Open the spreadsheet **BirthdayPG52L2**
- Use a VLOOKUP function in cell G3 that will look up a membership number entered by the receptionist in G2 and display the member's date of birth.

Formatting and design

In the test, you will need to show that you can use formatting such as bold, italics, underline, colour and borders to enhance your presentation. Make sure your presentation is clear and easy to read.

Formatting text

You can make titles and subtitles bold, large and different colours to make them stand out. Remember, the title should be larger than the subtitle.

You can use bullet points to break up the key information into smaller sections. Make sure bulleted text is large enough to be read from a distance – size 26 is a suitable size.

Golden rule

As in word-processing tasks, you should not use WordArt. Avoid using all capital letters (even for titles) as they can be difficult to read from a distance.

Formatting colour

You can add colourful borders and backgrounds to your slide show to make it look more eye-catching.

Make sure the colour of your text and background are suitable – choose either a light text on a dark background or a dark text on a light background.

Dinglewood Motors
Motoring specialist

Any questions?

Contact: Lorrayn Smith-Carterson
Telephone: 01632 431298
Email: lscarterson@dinglewood.bus.org

Consistent formatting

You should keep formatting consistent through your slide show. This means picking a colour scheme and using the same size text and style throughout.

Make sure your images are a sensible size. Unless the audience needs to read information on a chart or diagram, images are less important than the text.

Dinglewood Motors
Motoring specialist

This week only

- 10% discount on showroom prices
- Free services for 2 years
- Free tyre checks every 6 months

Now try this

- Open the file **IndiaPG67L2**
- Apply suitable formatting to make the presentation clear and easy to read.

Adding images

You can add images to a presentation to help to explain your ideas and to make your presentation more attractive. In the test, you may be given a selection of images to include in your slide show.

Inserting and editing images

Inserting images in Microsoft® PowerPoint works in exactly the same way as it does in Microsoft® Word. The same goes for copying, resizing, cropping and drawing shapes.

To avoid distorting an image when resizing it, use the 'Format Picture' tool.

 Right-click the image and choose 'Format Picture'.

 Click in the box next to 'Lock aspect ratio' so that a tick appears.

 Type the size you want your image to be in the height/width box and click OK.

Choosing the right images

Read the task to work out how many images you need to insert and where to insert them. Don't be tempted to add more images than you are asked for.

The image you put on each slide should relate to the bulleted text. You could be given an image in the test that isn't relevant, so you need to choose carefully.

Placing images

Choosing the 'Two Content' layout in Microsoft® PowerPoint allows you to easily place an image on one side of the slide, alongside the text.

Select the slide you want to add the image to. Click the 'Insert' tab, then add an image, clipart or shape.

Alternatively, you can drag the image file from the folder and drop it into the slide.

Inserting logos

You could be asked to insert a logo in the same position on every slide. The most efficient way to do this is to add the logo to the **Slide Master**.

 On the 'View' tab, click 'Slide Master'.

 Click on the slide at the very top of the 'slide panel'. You'll need to scroll up to see it. Anything you add to this 'master' slide will appear on all of your slides.

 Insert the logo on this slide.

 Click 'Close Master View' or select 'Normal' on the 'View' tab.

Now try this

- Open the presentation **IndiaPG68L2** and the folder **ImagesPG68L2**
- Add the logo to every slide.
- Add one suitable image to slides 2-5.

Adding audio and video

In the test, you could be asked to insert an audio (sound) file or video clip into your presentation.

Inserting an audio file

In the test, you could be given an audio file to include in your presentation.

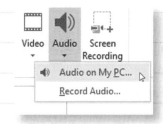

1 Go to the slide where you want to add the audio file. Go to the 'Insert' tab, then click 'Audio' and choose 'Audio on My PC'.

2 You will be supplied with an audio file with the image files. Select the audio file in the folder. Double-click the file to insert it.

3 A speaker icon will appear on the slide. You can resize and move this icon in the same way as an image.

> Sound files will usually end in .mp3, .wav or .wma.
> Video files will usually end in .mp4, .avi, .mov or .mpg.

Inserting a video file

In the test, you could be given a video file to include in your presentation.

1 Go to the slide where you want to add the video file. Go to the 'Insert' tab, then click 'Video' and choose 'Video on my PC'.

2 You will be supplied with a video file with the image files. Select the video file in the folder. Double-click the file to insert it.

3 If the slide is formatted as a 'Two Content' layout, the video will appear on one side. On a blank slide template, it will fill the whole slide. You can make a video appear smaller by clicking and dragging the corners, in the same way you would resize an image.

> To remove a video or audio file from a slide, click the video or the speaker icon and press 'Delete' on your keyboard. This doesn't delete the video file from the computer, it just removes it from the slide show.

Now try this

- Open the presentation **RelaxationPG69L2**
- Insert the sound file **BirdsPG69L2** and move the icon to a suitable position.
- Insert the video **NaturePG69L2** and place it in a suitable position.
- Save the file with a suitable name.

Transitions and animations

You might need to use simple slide **transitions** or **animations** in the test.

Transitions

Transitions are special effects that change the way slides appear on screen. Without transitions, each new slide appears suddenly.

Adding transitions

1 Click the 'Transitions' tab.

2 Choose a style. Click 'Apply to All' to put the same transition on all the slides.

3 In the slide panel, a star symbol will appear on every slide that has a transition applied to it.

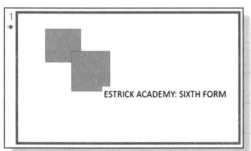

Animations

Animations let you control how and when text and images in a slide appear on the screen.

Adding animations

1 Click the 'Animations' tab.

2 Select the text or image to animate.

3 Choose an animation effect, such as 'Fade'.

Using timing

Bullets points can appear one-by-one, either automatically or when you click. To do this, you use the 'Timing' panel. Select 'On Click' or 'After Previous'.

A small number in an orange box will appear next to the text or image. This tells you what order the animation will happen in.

Evidence

In the test you may be asked for a screen shot to show you've added transitions or animations.

- For transitions, click the 'Transitions' tab and take a screen shot of the whole screen. The little star by each slide in the slide panel shows you have added a transition and the ribbon shows which one you've used.

- For animations, click the the 'Animations' tab. Click the image you animated to show which animation you used on the ribbon. Take a screen shot of your whole screen.

Now try this

- Open the presentation **FestivalPG70L2**
- Apply a transition of your choice to all slides.
- Apply an animation to the car image.
- Produce a screen shot showing that you've done both.

Checking and final touches

When you have completed the task, you should spend some time checking your presentation from start to finish.

Things to check

 Text

Read the text in your slide show carefully.

Remember to maximise the Microsoft® Notepad window to check you have included all the text.

- Have you copied across all the text correctly?
- Does every page have a title?
- Have you corrected any spelling mistakes?
- Does the information you've added (e.g. from your internet search or spreadsheet) make sense?
- Have you accidentally left in any guidance from the text file, such as 'Title' or 'Slide 2'?

 Images

Look back at the task instructions about images and logos.

- Have you inserted the correct number of images?
- Are the images placed with the text that they're related to?
- Have you included a logo on every page (if needed)?
- Have you distorted any of the images when you resized them?

Go to page 68 to revise adding images and logos.

 Formatting

Check that the formatting you have used is consistent throughout your slide show presentation.

- Is the bulleted text large enough to read from a distance (size 24 or larger)?
- Are the main title, subtitle and slide titles larger than the bullet text? Are they bold?
- Is there a good contrast between the font colour and any background colour?
- Do you have a colour scheme that links every slide?

 Adding headers and footers

In the test, you will be asked to include your name, candidate number and centre number in the footer of documents you edit or produce.

1. Click the 'Insert' tab, then select 'Header and Footer'.
2. Tick the box next to 'Footer' and type your details in the box beneath.
3. Click 'Apply to All'. The details will then appear at the bottom of every slide, including any new ones you add.

Now try this

The presentation **HealthyEatingPG71L2** will be displayed in the reception area of a nursery to tell parents about the Healthy Eating Day.

- Open the presentation.
- Identify **five** improvements that could be made to make it clear, easy to read and fit for purpose.

Slide show and print options

In the test, you won't be showing your presentation to an audience, but you need to be able to see what it would look like. You could be asked to print your slides, so make sure you are familiar with all of the options.

Printing slides

If you are asked to print slides, click 'File' and choose 'Print'.

If you choose 'Print All Slides', each slide will print out full size on a separate sheet.

You can also click the drop-down menu and choose to print just the slide you're looking at, or specific ones.

Printing handouts

In the test, you could be given a scenario where you need to print hand outs for an audience. For these, you'll probably want several slides on each page.

Click the drop-down menu next to 'Full Page Slides' to see the options. Some of them will provide space next to the slides for the audience to take notes.

Playing a slide show

To play your slide show, click the 'Slide Show' tab.

You can run your show from the beginning or from whichever slide you have on screen.

Click anywhere on the screen to move to the next slide. If you have added transitions, you will be able to see what these look like.

After the last slide, you'll see a black screen: click to return to the normal view.

Now try this

- Open the file **FestivalPG72L2**
- Set up the print options to print handouts three-per-page – you don't have to print for this practice.
- Make the file read-only. Produce a screen shot as evidence.

Remember to save a copy of the file before you make it read-only.

Putting it into practice

In the test, you could be asked to create a presentation using a Microsoft® Notepad file of text and a folder of images. You could also be asked to insert a video or audio file.

Estrick Hotel are promoting some seasonal offers and the manager would like you to produce a short presentation to be displayed in the hotel reception area. You've been given a Microsoft® Notepad file, **HotelOffersPG73L2**, with some text to use, and a folder of images, **ImagesPG73L2**

Create the presentation, enter your name in the footer on each slide, then save the presentation with a relevant file name.

The presentation must:

• have 6 slides

• be clear and easy to read

• have a consistent format

• be fit for purpose and audience.

It must include:

• relevant text from the file **HotelOffersPG73L2**

• the logo from **ImagesPG73L2** on each slide

• **one** appropriate image on each of slides 2–5 selected from **ImagesPG73L2**

• this information:

  • offers only valid for stays of 2 nights or more

• transitions on every slide.

Check the Microsoft® Notepad text carefully for errors, such as spelling mistakes and text that shouldn't be there. Remember that the folder of images might contain files that you don't need.

You can use the bullet points in the question as a checklist when you create your presentation.

Remember to follow the instructions exactly – if the question asks for one image then don't add more than that!

Evidence

A copy of your presentation saved on your desktop.

(18 marks)

Answers

GETTING STARTED

1 Preparing for your test

There is no model answer for this task. Make sure you are confident with this topic. Ask your teacher for help if you need additional support.

2 The basics

A scanner

3 Problem-solving

There is no model answer for this task. Make sure you are confident with this topic. Ask your teacher for help if you need additional support.

4 Settings and accessibility

Your answer could include two of the following:

- high contrast theme
- the magnifier
- the Narrator.

5 Health and safety

Your answer could include six of the following:

- no food and drink near the computer
- no clutter under your desk
- check your posture – feet flat on the floor
- take regular breaks
- wear glasses if you need them
- adjust your screen to avoid glare.

6 Files and folders

There is no model answer for this task. Make sure you are confident with this topic. Ask your teacher for help if you need additional support.

7 Keeping your information safe

1. Viruses and adware
2. Via email or on a shared network
3. EsTr1ckCO1

8 Putting it into practice:

1. Input device – your answer could include:
   - a keyboard
   - a mouse
   - a microphone.

   Output device – your answer could include:
   - a printer
   - a monitor
   - headphones.

   Input and output device – your answer could include:
   - an interactive whiteboard.

2. Click the undo button.
3. Any three of:
   - install antivirus software
   - make sure your computer automatically installs security updates
   - don't download files from untrustworthy websites
   - don't open attachments in suspicious emails.

4. Any two of the following:
   - a mixture of letters, numbers and symbols
   - contain both upper case and lower case letters
   - at least 8 characters
   - easy for you to remember but not easy for others to guess.

5. The Narrator reads aloud the options in dialogue boxes.

6.
   - If you want to send a large file by email.
   - So the files take up less space, for example on a USB stick or to upload to a website.

THE INTERNET

9 The internet

1.
   - The URL might be wrong. Ask your friend to check and resend the link.
   - You might not be connected to the internet. Check your internet connection.

10 Navigating a website

There is no model answer for this task. Make sure you are confident with this topic. Ask your teacher for help if you need additional support.

11 Searching for information

Open the file **AnswerPG11L2** to compare your screen shot with the model answer.

12 Searching for images

1.
   - A copy of the image in the 'Responses' document.
   - The website address of the image.

2.
   - Right-click the image.
   - Select 'Copy Image'.
   - Paste it into the 'Responses' document.

13 Evaluating information

(a) Circuses in Manchester Throughout History – No, not relevant as it would be about circuses in the past.

(b) Save our City Blog: Stop the Circus – No, likely to be biased against the circus and unlikely to give information about buying tickets.

(c) Foxtail Circus: 2013 show a sell-out! – No, not up-to-date.

(d) The Manchester Visitor Information Centre – Yes, should be reliable, objective, up-to-date and relevant.

14 Staying legal

Any three of the following:

- make sure that all personal information stored is up-to-date and relevant
- protect the data with a password so that only authorised people can see it
- check that no personal comments are stored, as the customer can ask to see the record
- never put the data on a removable storage device, as it could be lost or stolen.

15 Putting it into practice

1. Open the file **AnswerPG15L2** to compare your screen shot with the model answer.

2. Any three of the following:
   - the source is reliable
   - the source is objective
   - the source is relevant
   - the information is up-to-date.

EMAIL

16 What is email?

Any three advantages:

- Mitsuko can send one email to all 30 plumbers: much quicker than making 30 phone calls.
- There will be no cost involved.
- Nobody could argue that they were told it was another day, as it's in writing.
- Mitsuko could attach the agenda for the meeting.

Any three disadvantages:

- Some of the plumbers may not check their email in time.
- Some may not have an internet connection.
- Mitsuko might not know whether they have read the email or not.

17 Sending and receiving emails

Open the file **AnswerPG17L2** to compare your screen shot with the model answer.

18 Email contacts

- Cc
- To
- Bcc

19 Searching and sorting

Your answer could include either of the following:

- sort the inbox by date, oldest first, then do a search for Joanna
- sort by sender, then by date and scroll down to find Joanna.

20. Organising emails

1. Create a folder for emails from the Managing Director, set up a rule diverting all emails from her into it, and check it every day.

2. Important emails could be treated as junk, and if your junk email was deleted automatically every week they might be deleted before you had seen them.

21. Getting emails right

Open the file **AnswerPG21L2** to compare your screen shot with the model answer.

22 Email risks

Your answer could include any of these responses:

- a phishing email could trick you into entering your login details. Never go to your bank or other payment sites by clicking a link in an email. Go directly to the site using their web address instead

- links and attachments in emails could install a virus in your computer. Don't open programmes attached to emails or click a link without checking with the sender that they have sent it themselves. It could be from a fake email account

- think carefully about what you put in an email as it could be forwarded to others

- emails asking for money may be scams. Don't respond to any email asking for your bank details

- if you send an email about something urgent, the other person might not read it. You could text or phone to alert them.

23 Email troubleshooting

Any two of the following:

- Upload the files to a cloud storage site and send your colleague a link to access them.
- Zip them – this might make them small enough to send by email.

24 Putting it into practice

Open the file **AnswerPG24L2** to compare your screen shot with the model answer.

COMMUNICATE AND COLLABORATE

25 Online tools.

You could use a cloud-based storage tool and give them all access to the file so they can work on it together.

26 Safe and savvy online

- Change his privacy settings so that only his friends can see his posts and photos.
- Delete the post with his mobile number and send it by private message instead.

27 Putting it into practice

1. Google Drive™ (or any other cloud-storage service). You could upload the video and then share a link to it with your manager.

2. Skype® (or any other video chat services). People all over the world can communicate using this type of online tool at any time for free.

3. Your answer could include any two of the following:
   - have strong passwords on your social media accounts
   - only make friends with people you know in real life
   - don't put personal details on your public profile
   - use privacy settings to make sure only your friends can see your posts and profile
   - use the junk filter on your email account to remove any suspicious messages.

WORD PROCESSING

28 Entering text

Open the file **AnswerPG28L2** to see the model answer.

29 Formatting text

Open the file **AnswerPG29L2** to see the model answer.

30 Page layout

Open the file **AnswerPG30L2** to see the model answer.

Answers

31 Using tables
Open the file **AnswerPG31L2** to see the model answer.

32 Using images
Open the file **AnswerPG32L2** to see the model answer.

33 Using text boxes and shapes
Open the file **AnswerPG33L2** to see the model answer.

34 Audience and Purpose
Your answer could include any six of the following:

- change the border to a plain box
- Word-Art is not suitable for a business document: format the heading large and bold
- remove the underlining from the Present and Apologies section – it doesn't improve clarity
- make the headings **Present** and **Apologies** bold
- font sizes should be consistent, e.g. 22pt for main heading, 16pt for subheadings, 12-14pt for body text
- the supplier issues paragraph should be left-aligned like the rest
- no text language: 'Sam will fone him 2 arrange a visit.' should read 'Sam will phone him to arrange a visit.'
- no emoticons – remove the smiley
- adjust to fit on one page if there are just a couple of lines on page 2.

35 Posters and adverts
Open the file **AnswerPG35L2** to see the model answer.

36 Newsletters, leaflets and flyers
Open the file **AnswerPG36L2** to see the model answer.

37 Letters and business documents
Open the file **AnswerPG37L2** to see the model answer.

38 Checking your work
Open the file **AnswerPG38L2** to see the model answer.

39 Putting it into practice
Open the file **AnswerPG39L2** to see the model answer.

SPREADSHEETS

40 Understanding spreadsheets
Open the file **AnswerPG40L2** to see a model answer.

41 Entering and changing data
Open the file **AnswerPG41L2** to see a model answer.

42 Rows and columns
Open the file **AnswerPG42L2** to see a model answer.

43 Formatting data
Open the file **AnswerPG43L2** to see a model answer.

44 Using simple formulas
Open the file **AnswerPG44L2** to see a model answer.

45 Using SUM, MIN and MAX
Open the file **AnswerPG45L2** to see a model answer.

46 Averages
Open the file **AnswerPG46L2** to see a model answer.

47 Finding percentages
Open the file **AnswerPG47L2** to see a model answer.

48 Relative and absolute cell references
Open the file **AnswerPG48L2** to see a model answer.

49 Tracking balances
Open the file **AnswerPG49L2** to see a model answer.

50 Conditional formatting
Open the file **AnswerPG50L2** to see a model answer.

51 Using IF
Open the file **AnswerPG51L2** to see a model answer.

52 Using VLOOKUP
Open the file **AnswerPG52L2** to see a model answer.

53 Sorting
Open the file **AnswerPG53L2** to see a model answer.

54 Using filters
Open the file **AnswerPG54L2** to see a model answer.

55 Viewing and printing formulas
Open the file **AnswerPG55L2** to see a model answer.

56 Putting it into practice
Open the file **AnswerPG56L2** to see a model answer.

CHARTS AND GRAPHS

57 Types of chart and graph
A column or bar chart because there is more than one set of data to compare.

58 Selecting data
- The 'Total' column has been included.
- The column headings have not been selected.
- The chart title hasn't been updated.

59 Creating a pie chart
Open the file **AnswerPG59L2** to see a model answer.

60 Creating a bar chart
Open the file **AnswerPG60L2** to see a model answer.

61 Creating a line graph
Open the file **AnswerPG61L2** to see a model answer.

62 Formatting charts and graphs
Open the file **AnswerPG62L2** to see a model answer.

63 Including charts in other documents
Open the file **AnswerPG63L2** to see a model answer.

64 Putting it into practice
Open the file **AnswerPG64L2** to see a model answer.

65 Understanding presentations

Your answer could include any five of the following:

- the font on the title slide is too small
- the logo is too large and hides part of the title
- Slide 2 has far too much information on; it's very cluttered
- the fonts on Slide 2 are too small
- the content of Slide 2 could not be seen from a distance
- the information on Slide 2 is a flyer and should have been produced using word-processing software
- the background of Slide 2 is too dark and makes the text hard to read
- Slide 3 does not provide any information. There should be contact details or some other instruction, or thanks for help.

66 Creating a presentation

Open the file **AnswerPG66L2** to see a model answer.

These are the three mistakes to correct:

1. India is in South Asia and has the second largest population in the world.
2. Originally built as a mausoleum for his favourite wife…
3. There are miles **of** sandy beaches.

67 Formatting and design

Open the file **AnswerPG67L2** to see a model answer.

68 Adding images

Open the file **AnswerPG68L2** to see a model answer.

69 Adding audio and video

Open the file **AnswerPG69L2** to see a model answer.

70 Transitions and animation

Open the file **AnswerPG70L2** to see a model answer.

71 Checking and final touches

Your answer could include any five of the following:

- choose a lighter background colour
- move the logo to the Slide Master so that it appears on every slide
- correct the distortion of the stretched clock image
- remove the text 'Title' from the title slide
- increase the size of the font.

72 Slide show and print options

Open the file **AnswerPG72L2** to see a model answer.

73 Putting it into practice

Open the file **AnswerPG73L2** to see a model answer.

Published by Pearson Education Limited, 80 Strand, London, WC2R 0RL.

www.pearsonschoolsandfecolleges.co.uk

Copies of official specifications for all Edexcel qualifications may be found on the website: www.edexcel.com

Text © Pearson Education Limited 2016
Edited, typeset and produced by Elektra Media Ltd
Original illustrations © Pearson Education Limited 2016
Illustrated by Elektra Media Ltd
Cover illustration by Miriam Sturdee

First published 2016

19 18 17 16
10 9 8 7 6 5 4 3 2 1

British Library Cataloguing in Publication Data
A catalogue record for this book is available from the British Library

ISBN 978 1 292 14593 8

Printed in Italy by Lego S.p.A.

All images © Pearson Education